HERO OF YOUR LIFE

*How to
Get Unstuck,
Move Forward
and Live Your
True Authentic Life*

J. SCOTT MACMILLAN

BALBOA
PRESS

A DIVISION OF HAY HOUSE

Balboa Press books may be ordered through booksellers or by contacting:

Balboa Press
A Division of Hay House
1663 Liberty Drive
Bloomington, IN 47403
www.balboapress.com
1 (877) 407-4847

Because of the dynamic nature of the Internet, any web addresses or links contained in this book may have changed since publication and may no longer be valid. The views expressed in this work are solely those of the author and do not necessarily reflect the views of the publisher, and the publisher hereby disclaims any responsibility for them.

The author of this book does not dispense medical advice or prescribe the use of any technique as a form of treatment for physical, emotional, or medical problems without the advice of a physician, either directly or indirectly. The intent of the author is only to offer information of a general nature to help you in your quest for emotional and spiritual well-being. In the event you use any of the information in this book for yourself, which is your constitutional right, the author and the publisher assume no responsibility for your actions.

Any people depicted in stock imagery provided by Getty Images are models, and such images are being used for illustrative purposes only. Certain stock imagery © Getty Images.

Print information available on the last page.

ISBN: 978-1-9822-1642-9 (sc)
ISBN: 978-1-9822-1643-6 (hc)
ISBN: 978-1-9822-1644-3 (e)

Library of Congress Control Number: 2018913731

Balboa Press rev. date: 12/05/2018

CONTENTS

INTRODUCTION

In the summer of 2001, I was in the shower when I suddenly heard a voice in my head that said, "This is not the way to live life--you must be doing something wrong." Life had just spiraled out of control. Here, I was living in a beautiful house in a great city with a wife, two healthy children and a good corporate job, yet I was miserable. My health was failing, my marriage was falling apart, and my job had become stagnate and unfulfilling. I was simply going through the motions of life.

That morning, I wanted the hot water to unwind my extremely painful back and neck muscles. About a year prior, I had noticed that my right shoulder ached after having played catch with my son, so I made what would become the first of many physical therapy and doctor appointments. The pain just kept getting worse, and was spreading through my back with each new doctor or physical therapist I saw. I was exhausted and in constant chronic pain. By that morning in the shower, I had not only tried traditional doctors but a whole host of alternative therapies, including cortisone shots, physical therapy, acupuncture, red light laser therapy, as well as massage and chiropractic.

After the first inkling that something was off with how I was living my life, it would be over 15 years later when I realized that the voice I had heard that morning was my calling to my first Hero's Journey. Little did I know it would be one of the most significant days of my life. It was the day I woke up, and focused internally and stopped blaming the outside world for my problems. I had no clue what to do, but I knew I first needed to change my thoughts before I could heal, and live a healthy and fulfilling life again.

Millions of people suffer from lack-luster, non-fulfilling lives. Anxiety disorders are the most common mental illness in the United States. According to the Anxiety and Depression Association of America (ADAA), 40 million Americans over the age of 18 are affected by anxiety.

Fear. A survey reported that many CEOs of billion dollar companies had the fear that "someday I'll be found out and they'll take it all away from me."

Stress is up. Most Americans are suffering from moderate to high stress, with 44 percent reporting that their stress levels have increased over the past five years. Concerns about money, work and the economy top the list of most frequently cited sources of stress.

Lack of willpower. People cite lack of willpower as the biggest barrier to adopting healthier behaviors. But 70 percent of these people believe that willpower is something they can learn or improve if only they had more money, energy or confidence in their ability to change.

Fear, anxiety, stress, lack of willpower, and low self-esteem are holding us back from achieving our dreams. We feel stuck and stagnate and know there is more out there for us.

Ordinary people like you and me suffer from living in stuck and stagnate states.

- Jim had become a wealthy entrepreneur, but he had a hard time enjoying his business success because it seemed that every minute he wasn't solving a business problem he was worried about what others thought of him and what he could do to get their approval.
- Janelle had many good ideas, but because she was plagued with procrastination, she was nowhere near as successful as she could have been.
- Steven always talked about his dream of doing something on his own, but he just didn't have the confidence to leave his safe but boring job.

- And finally there is Cindy, who complained of bouts of anxiety that seemed to come over her without warning and paralyze her.

Stories like these go on forever. I've heard many of them. It seems as if no one really escapes having a low sense of self-esteem, a negative sense of oneself, or an inner voice that is constantly critical of oneself.

Anyone who knows there is more to life than what they are currently experiencing will want to read this book. Most people don't know how to get unstuck and move forward.

So, how did I do it? Well, this book will reveal that for you. This book is the final stage of my first Hero's Journey because as you will see, the journey ends with the sharing of your story to others, thereby helping them identify their own story and thus, begin the process of healing and living their true authentic lives. And then we start our next one.

I stumbled upon the "Hero's Journey" concept as I was studying documentary filmmaking. It was originally attributed to the mythologist Joseph Campbell, but has been refined by many authors and scholars to depict a common theme used in all stories and movies. As you will see, by using Campbell's initial concept of a Hero's Journey as a map of your own life, you will understand who you truly are and that you've always been the hero in your own life story. Learning about what makes us tick enhances our self-motivation and self-management, resulting in self-respect.

My story may or may not resonate with you, but I like to think that it will to some extent, because I am just a normal guy with a family and with a normal life. In contrast to some, I didn't have a traumatic childhood, as I was born and raised in a nice middle-class neighborhood in Montana. A self-help junkie, I have seen my share of personal development stories – some of the heroic journeys that individuals have gone through are genuinely inspiring. When I compare them with my own life story, I'm embarrassed as I have nothing for which to complain about and that my suffering pales in comparison to theirs. On the other hand, through my journey I learned that putting myself down and comparing myself to others is a limiting belief that I've carried for years. Nevertheless, I feel there may be a lot of us who have had nice lives, yet still get stuck and suffer. True, we all suffer; but some have the capacity to let things go and forge on, while others can't. I feel fortunate to have been at the right time and the right place in my life to take my suffering, and transmute it into understanding and healing. It's my hope that through my story, you will realize you are a hero and that you will answer the call to take your own Hero's Journey, thereby finding health, happiness and a fulfilling, purpose-driven life.

How to Use This Book

As we dissect the stages of the Hero's Journey and map them to the stages of human development, you will be able to place yourself into your own Hero's Journey. You will learn to identify how your life has been influenced by each stage of the journey, and where in your life you have identified with the hero. This will help you heal and move through the stages. Finally, understanding that we have done the best we could at the time allows us be the hero of our own lives. You see, when we realize that our life has been in service for us, we begin to feel empowered to take risks, start trusting our internal guidance and truly live our best authentic life.

In addition to understanding and healing, you will also learn powerful guided meditations and complete thought-provoking exercises to help you fully integrate the lessons learned on your journey. These exercises and tools are designed to help you fully heal and understand past traumas as you move from one stage to the next. We will also explore ancient principles of human thought and consciousness to help us recognize that how we think dictates how we live. Once you know the path of your Hero's Journey, you will need to apply the latest research on living genuinely extraordinary lives. We 'll dive into the amazing scientific work of Dr. Joe Dispenza and his Quantum Thinking model, where we will learn to train our brains to think differently.

If you've been stuck or feel there is more to life, it's most likely because you've been focusing on symptoms instead of getting to the root cause of your suffering. Learning your own Hero's Journey will help you discover why you're stuck, and help you heal and move forward so you can begin living your true authentic and purposeful life.

The only difference between people who are truly abundant and thriving in all areas of life and those who are stuck and stagnate, is that the former have heard the call to adventure and stepped out of their comfortable, ordinary world to begin walking forward into their Hero's Journey.

Answering the call and moving from your ordinary life into the unknown is not only the thing you fear the most but it's real work. And it's hard--but you can do it. You know you must do it.

> *"The cave you fear to enter holds the treasure you seek."*
> *- Joseph Campbell*

You have a deep understanding that there is something of more significance for you and you're finally ready to figure it out. To find and live your true authentic life though, you've got to wander through the desert of your traumas. You've got to get to the root cause of what's kept you stuck and be more honest then you probably have ever been with yourself. You've got to face your biggest fear, stare it right in the face and walk through it. This is serious work that will pay off the highest rewards this life has to offer. It will not be easy, you will want to quit, and you will make a lot of mistakes. It's going to be messy and scary. But that's okay. Don't give up--stay with this process and see it through. Your life depends on it.

For downloadable PDF exercises and videos on Being Your Own Hero visit www.betheheroofyourlife.com/downloads

SECTION ONE
THE HERO'S JOURNEY

CHAPTER 1
WHAT IS THE HERO'S JOURNEY?

So, what is the Hero's Journey? It can mostly be traced to Joseph Campbell, an American scholar and mythologist. Campbell identified a basic narrative that appears in drama, storytelling, myth, religious ritual, and personal development. He studied all the indigenous and cultural myths and stories of the world, and found there is one main storyline that exists within all of them: It describes the typical adventure of the archetype known as "The Hero."

In his study of the archetypal myth of the hero, Campbell suggests the existence of a Monomyth, a universal pattern that is the essence of, and common to, heroic tales in every culture. The main character, the hero, goes out and achieves great deeds on behalf of himself, a group, or civilization. Many writers, as well as popular movies like *The Wizard of Oz, Star Wars, Superman, The Godfather, Titanic and Avatar* -- have used the framework of the Hero's Journey. The character archetypes we see in our modern action hero movies are basically contemporary versions of ancient myths.

Campbell's classic version has three main parts.

Departure: The hero is in one form of reality, then is suddenly separated from it. The hero receives a call to action, gains a mentor, and learns of their destiny.

Initiation: The hero comes into their own, faces and overcomes problems, then finally meets their match and receives a renewed sense of purpose.

Return: The hero accepts their responsibility, gains some magical help, slays some dragons and returns home with treasure and stories.

I've adopted a more personal development depiction of the three main phases and have titled them The Preparation, The Journey and The Return. As you will see, the first four stages of the Hero's Journey prepare the hero for the main journey and return phases.

Great hero movies call on the hero within all of us when we watch them. For Dorothy in <u>The Wizard of Oz</u>, it wasn't just about defeating the wicked witch; it was about claiming her own inner resources. At the end of the movie, she realized she had the ability to get back home all along by clicking her heels; she just needed to go through the trials and tribulations to come to that realization.

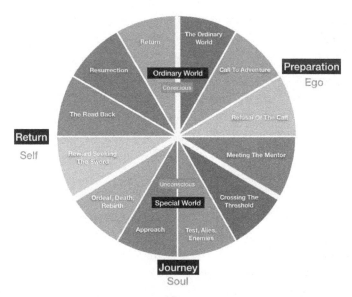

THIS GRAPHIC SHOWS THE 12 STAGES OF THE HERO'S JOURNEY. THE JOURNEY IS DEPICTED AS A CIRCLE BECAUSE THE HERO MUST ALWAYS

RETURN TO BRING BOTH THE TREASURE OF THE VICTORY HOME AND THE STORIES SO OTHERS MAY FIND AND PARTAKE IN THEIR OWN HERO'S JOURNEY. IT ALSO LISTS THE THREE MAIN PHASES (PREPARATION, JOURNEY AND RETURN) AND HOW THEY LINE UP WITH CARL JUNG'S PERSONAL DEVELOPMENTAL MODEL OF THE EGO, SOUL AND SELF. IN ADDITION, IT DELINEATES WHICH STAGES ARE IN THE ORDINARY OR SPECIAL WORLD.

The key to using the Hero's Journey as a light in our lives is to embrace metaphor. We've all heard the story about the knights of the round table and their epic search for the Holy Grail. The story is not about the grail itself; it's about the metaphor for that intangible feeling they are searching for. Metaphors instruct us on how to lead an extraordinary and fulfilling life by embedding wisdom and information within the content of the story.

Once we're taught about a mythical character, just thinking of that character invokes their entire story and its meaning. Carl Jung, one of the fathers of modern psychology, called these 'archetypes'. These are encapsulated stories that plant a seed in our collective consciousness. When that archetypal idea is planted, it starts to sprout. It brings forth the relationships and patterns that help unfold the story we are journeying through. According to Jung, the collective consciousness is the repository of all symbols and experiences of religion, spirituality, and mythology. These archetypal images are ingrained in our understanding before birth, and they become the conceptual patterns behind all our thinking and beliefs.

It's much easier to tell a story to help explain life than just simply giving an explanation. Stories are richer and move deeper into our psyche. So, it's possible to follow these hero stories, see ourselves in them, and therefore manifest the reality of the hero moving through the journey to reap the reward. In mythology, the Hero's Journey chronicles the notion that all mystical traditions call us to a deeper understanding of the act of living itself. Myths and stories guide us through trials and traumas from birth to death.

We are all capable of finding meaning and purpose in our lives, and in the Hero's Journey, we find a model for learning how to live in stories about heroism. The Hero's Journey is about saying yes to yourself and becoming more fully alive and effective in the world. The Hero's Journey is mainly about taking a journey to find the treasure of your authentic self, and then about returning home to tell your story to help transform the kingdom, village or community you inhabit, and in the process, your own life. The journey is fraught with dangers like metaphorical dragons and ogres that we must slay so we can reap the rewards of the knowledge we can gain by finding our unique gifts. We never stop journeying. Each time we begin our journey, we do so at a new level and return with new treasure and newfound transformative abilities. Thus, the Hero's Journey coming full-circle.

Hero's come in all shape and sizes. Some are adventurous, while others shun the hero label. Some start out weak, some start strong. Some are family-oriented, while others are loners. Heroes are far from perfect; they have flaws like we all do. The essence of what makes a hero though, is the willingness to serve others and give themselves to the greater good.

Campbell talks about following your bliss as the essence to the Hero's Journey. To follow your bliss means to follow your heart and follow your truth. According to Campbell, bliss is not ecstasy or happiness. There is a serenity in bliss. It's the thing that you can't not do. It's your authentic self, calling you to find your soul's life purpose and live in it. It's about doing what makes us feel most alive. Embarking on your Hero's Journey is to have the courage to look within and ask yourself, what am I here to do? What am I most passionate about in my life? What are my greatest gifts, and how do I give them to the world?

> "Life has no meaning. Each of us has meaning and we bring it to life. It is a waste to be asking the question when you are the answer."
>
> ~ Joseph Campbell

After coming across the Hero's Journey concept, I mapped my life to the stages and began to see how my life unfolded in perfect compatibility with the hero movies and stories I'd seen. Once I realized I was the hero of my life, I finally had the courage and motivation to make my life truly extraordinary by facing my fears and unleashing years of pent-up and trapped emotions. I wrote this book to be used as a framework to help people in all stages of life's journey, whether they are just beginning or as a reference for longtime journeyers. Through my own journey, I've found many tools and exercises that have helped me and my clients move through the stages of the journey with greater awareness and ease. When we learn about the many different heroic paths available to us, we begin to understand there is hope for us to be our own heroes.

Stories about heroes link our own path with those who have come before us in such a way that we learn something about what it means to be human. As we explore the stages of the Hero's Journey, we'll look at some popular movies and see how they match up with Campbell's stages and how they can be used as examples of ordinary people becoming heroes. I'll also share the stages of my Hero's Journey so you can emulate me to the path of healing.

CHAPTER 2
JUNG'S DEVELOPMENTAL MODEL - THE EGO, THE SOUL, AND THE SELF

The three phases of the Hero's Journey that I mentioned above – preparation, journey and return, line up perfectly with Carl Jung's Developmental Model which he called the Individuation Model of personal development: the ego, the soul and the self.

According to Jung, the ego shows us how to be safe and successful in the world, while the soul helps us become authentic as we explore the mysteries of life. The journey of the self illustrates how we can shine in our authenticity, power, and freedom.

In the first stage of preparation, the ego comes directly into play, as the time when the hero prepares to leave the comfortable and stable environment and develops the inner resources necessary to go out into the world on their own. On the journey, the hero discovers their true gifts. The return is when the hero returns to the community to share these gifts and live with others in a state of interdependence.

Carol Pearson, author of "Awakening The Hero's Within" explains Jung's developmental model as such: "The Ego is the platform for our life. It creates the boundaries between us and everything else, and mediates our relationship with the world. It shows us how to fit into the world and to act to change that world to better meet our needs. The Soul connects us with the spiritual. It is also the pure potential of human beings, like seeds germinating and ready to sprout if external conditions are prosperous. The Self is our sense of our identity. When the Self is born, we finally know who we are; we experience wholeness and integrity. We then try to find ways to express ourselves in the world and in doing so, make contributions that only we alone can make to bring joy and authenticity to our lives."

As we explore the Hero's Journey and map it to Jung's developmental model, we can see, as the table below shows, the basic healthy developmental tasks and outcomes that are achieved from each developmental stage (ego, soul, self). For example, when we move from the ego stage to the soul stage, a healthy ego should have established caring for ourselves and caring for others. Therefore, as we study and explore our own developmental stages, we may find we need healing work in our ego stage before we can truly move into our soul and self stages.

Once we have reviewed and identified ourselves in this formula, we can begin to see where understanding and healing needs to occur so that we can claim the treasure of living as our true authentic self and find our purpose in life.

Stage of The Journey	Preparation	Journey	Return
Human Development	Ego	Soul	Self
Outcome	Caring for the self and getting along with others	Finding your gifts, values and purpose	Sharing your gifts with others and living in integrity

Developmental Tasks	Trust Developing trust in self and others **Autonomy -** Standing up for, protecting and defending the self **Initiative -** Learning to take responsibility for yourself **Industry -** Learning basic social skills and work habits	Identity Finding what you love and creating and letting go **Intimacy** Finding whom you love and willingness to commit and let go	Generatively Actively sharing your gifts with others **Intimacy** Being true to yourself and claiming your own wisdom
Stages of the Hero's Journey	The Ordinary World The Call to Adventure Refusal of The Call Meeting the Mentor	Crossing the Threshold Test, Allies & Enemies The Approach The Ordeal	The Reward The Road Back The Resurrection Return with The Treasure

Adapted from Patricia R. Adson and Carol S. Pearson

Before we look at the stages of the Hero's Journey, let's make sure we understand and adapt the myth, story and movie structure of outer world conquests, to the inner journey of personal development. For the purposes of self-discovery, we no longer want to view the Hero's Journey map as a representation of a physical place. We want to go inside ourselves and uncover our true authentic and purpose-driven life by understanding our feelings and emotions and how they have contributed to our life so far.

Referring to the 12 stages of the Hero's Journey and the division of the ordinary world from the special world, it's helpful to equate our conscious mind with the ordinary world (the known), and our unconscious mind with the special world (the unknown). These subtle changes enable us to adapt Campbell's mythically-based Hero's Journey from stories and movies, to personal growth and development.

CHAPTER 3
PHASE I - PREPARATION FOR THE JOURNEY

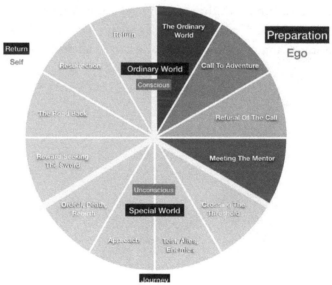

THE HERO'S JOURNEY PREPARATION MAP

In the preparation phase, the first four stages of Campbell's Hero's Journey are The Ordinary World, The Call to Adventure, Refusal of The Call, and Meeting the Mentor. These four stages represent preparation for the journey ahead. When we compare the stages of the Hero's Journey to that of Jung's first developmental stage, we see that the Ego teaches us how to be safe and successful in the world, which prepares us for our journey. The hero is often said to be the archetype of the Ego, but this is only partially true. The Hero's Journey encompasses all the developmental stages. Establishing a healthy Ego, however, is the prerequisite for taking the journey safely.

We come into this world, small, fragile, and helpless with our Ego unformed. We are left in the care of parents or other adults who try hard but don't always know what we need. As we gain control over our lives, we begin to learn what we can do and how we can affect what happens to us. With this awareness, the Ego is born.

Jung points out that no matter how old or wise or mature we are, we were all vulnerable little children who still bear the scars of our formative years. The Ego's first task is to protect the inner child. At some point during childhood, the ego begins to take on the protective function from the parent, and gradually with maturation, assumes that task completely. The Ego's next task, and its basic function, is to mediate our relationship with the outside world.

The stories we identify most with are those about Ego development. The classic hero on a white horse, the knight slaying the dragon, Luke Skywalker defeating Darth Vader are all versions of the classic story of the Ego. The hero and the kingdom are in danger from some hostile force. The key is having the courage and ability to defend the gates. The hero is often the conqueror, the man or woman who goes after what they want. Carol Pearson eloquently puts it this way: "The capacity to get what we want and protect our boundaries does not, in itself, make us heroes. What makes a hero is a nobility of spirit manifested as concern and compassion for others."

Pearson goes on to explain, "Preparation for the journey requires each of us to be socialized adequately, be effective in society and then separate from the world enough to assert independent values, opinions, and desires. Finally, it demands that we use this capacity for autonomy and independence, not simply for selfish ends - although we do want to seek our own good - we seek for the good of the whole as well."

Stage One: The Ordinary World

According to Campbell's theory, in stories and myth, the ordinary world is where the hero is introduced in a basic and sympathetic way so the audience can identify with the situation or dilemma. The ordinary world is the baseline; the status quo. It may not be pretty or exactly the way we want it, but for better or worse, this is where we're at right now. There is polarity though, in the hero's life that pulls him or her in different directions and causes stress. A hidden part of us hints at change, seeks a renewed spirit and foresees a better future.

We meet our first reluctant hero on a desert planet where he lives with his aunt and uncle who took him in after his father disappeared. As he does his daily chores of repairing and maintaining moisture farming droids, he longs for more. He stands on a bluff as the twin suns of Tatoonie are setting and gazes out on the horizon, wishing he could become a pilot and escape the dusty planet. In the 1977 movie, *Star Wars: A New Hope*, we are introduced to Luke Skywalker, played by Mark Hamel, who languishes in his ordinary world, knowing there is more for him. Joseph Campbell praised the movie's creator and director, George Lucas, as a master storyteller using all the classic stages of the Hero's Journey in his epic Star Wars movies.

My ordinary world was living in suburbia with my wife and kids and a good but stressful corporate job. We had just moved from northern Virginia where I was an engineer and corporate trainer. Life certainly appeared wonderful and was for the first three years in our new house in the burbs. My wife was able to stay home to raise the kids and I was climbing the corporate ladder. We had been married for eleven years at the time I had my morning shower voice experience, but what happened before that was what I call the 'blind time'. I was blindly following the American dream with my head down, working hard, raising kids and not paying attention to my stress levels, my body or anything other than striving to make the American dream come true--whatever that was. Don't get me wrong, it's not that I wasn't enjoying life. I was coaching my kids in sports and enjoying friends and family on the weekends and holidays, but all along, the stress monster was eating away at my mind and body, and I had no idea it was happening.

As Campbell explains, we are living in our present day but we are uneasy and uncomfortable and unaware. Unaware that there is something else out there waiting for us. Or that there is another way to behave or react to everyday events.

Campbell states "The Hero's home is the haven upon which the Special World and the Journey's outcome must be compared." The Journey begins in Stage One: the Ordinary World, then travels to the Special World, and returns to the Ordinary World. As we go through the Campbell's stages, remember that it's helpful to equate the Ordinary World with our conscious mind and the Special World with the subconscious mind. We start out living in our normal conscious mind world until something happens to us and we have to look inside at our subconscious mind to find the answers to why we are behaving a certain way.

Campbell also believes that most of us live with the illusion that the life we are living is all there is. For many of us, our lives are filled with media bombardment and consumerism. We are lured into a trance of comfort; not wanting to stick our heads out too far. So, as heroes, we are confronted with the fact that the reality we thought was real – consumerism and comfort – isn't real. Therefore, we must not be afraid to go within to find meaning and significance. In our contemporary "more is better" culture, spirituality and personal development are less appreciated, less valued and less understood than worshiping the outer displays of success.

Stage Two: The Call to Adventure

For the hero, separation from the illusion begins with stage two, The Call to Adventure. The phone is ringing. The Universe/God/Creator is literally calling you to step out and live your journey. Something breaks into your reality and makes it impossible for you to continue down your current path. You can ignore the call and not answer, but it will keep calling back until you finally answer the call.

For a lot of us, the wake-up call comes in the form of a sledgehammer. Often, it comes in the depths of our despair, losing a job, a health crisis (like me), getting divorced, dealing with foreclosure on your house, etc. These aren't the things you want to happen in your life, but they are exactly what you need to awaken and catapult you into the next phase of your journey. The Universe/God/Creator just upended you, knocked you on your ass and woke you up.

But here is the miracle in this. Your waking is the opportunity you've been waiting for; you just didn't know it. Did you know that the Chinese symbol of crisis is two symbols, one means danger and the other means opportunity? So, crisis be both danger and opportunity together.

Chinese symbol for crisis

A young boy is forced to sleep in a closet by his aunt and uncle and is constantly tortured by his bratty cousin. In the 2001 movie, *Harry Potter and the Sorcerer's Stone,* created by J.K. Rowling, we see Harry Potter, played by Daniel Radcliffe, in his gloomy ordinary world.

Harry's call to adventure came with a bang as the giant man known as Hagrid crashes through the door to personally deliver Harry a letter of acceptance from Hogwarts School of Witchcraft and Wizardry, where Harry's amazing adventures would begin.

My first inkling that something needed to change in my life started on a normal day. I wasn't feeling good that day; I wasn't feeling that good for many weeks, but that day I was feeling especially bad and very lethargic. I came home after work and tried to forget about everything and just get to the next day. I went to bed early but couldn't get to sleep, and at around 2 a.m., I woke my wife and told her I needed to go the emergency room because I was having a kidney stone attack. When I was in college, I had my first kidney stone but it was a gradual and slow, dull pain that would come and go. This started slow but came on strong, and I was sure this was an acute kidney stone attack. So, we loaded our kids – who were very young at the time – into the car, and headed to the emergency room. It felt like hours before the ER doctors could see me, run some tests and finally give me pain medication. By the time they wheeled me into the X-ray room, I was in excruciating pain and don't remember much of anything else until the next morning when I woke up in the hospital with a morphine drip and so thankful the pain was gone. I had passed the stone during the night and thought my problems and pain would soon to be over. Oh, was I wrong. They released me later that day and as the pain medication wore off, my stomach still hurt. Not the same kind of dull achy pain as the kidney stone, but more of a nauseous and stabbing pain that didn't go away for eight months. Those eight months consisted of seeing doctor after doctor and having test after test which showed no traditional signs for the way I was feeling. At that time, when they couldn't diagnose stomach problems, they just assumed it was irritable bowel syndrome. They now have some treatments for that, but at the time, they didn't have any. After trying every diet under the sun to alleviate my pain, as well as losing 25 pounds, the symptoms slowly got better on their own. But here's the kicker: I still didn't know what was going on with me and didn't understand the internal wisdom of the call to adventure that was trying to alert me to change my thinking and my life.

When my stomach pain couldn't get my attention, the divine wisdom in my body found other areas of weakness and trapped emotional trauma to exploit. We'll discuss how we all have trapped emotional trauma stuck in our body from the age of our infancy to around six years of age that affects our adult life in many ways later. Anyway, as I mentioned before, I was playing catch with my son one day when I noticed that my arm was particularly sore that night. That soreness grew into lots of pain that sent me back to the doctor to be examined. Once again, I was back on the treadmill of doctors, MRI's, physical therapists, injections in my neck and finally meetings with surgeons, all of who said I didn't need surgery to fix my back problems. I was getting close to hearing the call because at that point, I decided to stop seeing all doctors and just chill out. I began taking Tai Chi and Yoga classes and reading about stress reduction. This was the first inkling I had that I needed to reduce my stress and start living my life differently. But it wasn't until that morning in the shower, that I actually heard my first call to adventure.

In the classic movie, *The Wizard of Oz*, which debuted in 1939, Dorthy, played by Judy Garland, is called to adventure when her house falls on the wicked witch and she enters the land of Oz. She has no choice but to follow the yellow brick road (her Hero's Journey) to find the wizard and get back home. For most of us, our call to adventure is a feeling or a knowing that there is more; while for others, like Dorothy and Harry, the call is a big event that forces you to take your journey.

Stage Three: Refusal of The Call

Before we cross the threshold, most of us move into Stage Three, which is the Refusal of The Call. It's very common for the hero to feel the fear of the unknown and try to turn away from the adventure. Who hasn't experienced this? We have a feeling that we should make a change or do something that is out of our comfort zone, but we back away and push that thought out of our head because we are afraid. There are many reasons we refuse the call. We may not know ourselves well enough to recognize it, and even if we do, we may not be ready for it. We may not want it badly enough, or maybe we're not sure the call is for us. One thing is certain though, if we refuse the call, the Universe/God/Creator doesn't give up. We will constantly experience suffering and repeat these patterns until we finally answer the call and cross the threshold into the special world.

One of the funniest movie examples of refusing the call comes from the 1993 movie, *Groundhog Day*, where actor Bill Murray portrays Phil Conner's, a local news reporter who is repeatedly forced to relive a negative loop cycle of days, until he embraces the call and becomes a better person.

Who hasn't felt like Phil when he wakes up to the same alarm clock radio program and experiences the same day repeatedly. The Universe/God/Creator will continue to remind us that we need to change.

We see another great example of the refusal of the call in director James Cameron's classic 1997 movie, <u>Titanic</u>. Our hero, or heroine in this case, is Rose DeWitt Bukater, played by Kate Winslet, an English debutant who is to be married to the wealthy businessman Cal Hockley. Rose, who is distraught about the impending marriage, tries to jump off the ship, but a drifter named Jack Dawson, played by Leonardo DiCaprio, talks her off the ledge and they start a friendship. Rose's refusal of the call comes when Jack tries to convince her not to marry Cal and be with him. Rose insists that she'll be happy with Cal but she is only saying that because her mom wants Cal's money.

After the famous sunset kiss on the bow scene, we see another refusal of the call when Jack is arrested for allegedly stealing Rose's diamond necklace. She again refuses the call when she starts to doubt Jack's intentions and lets the authorities take him away in handcuffs. Of course, we know that she finally accepts the call to adventure when she jumps off the lifeboat to be with Jack as the Titanic tragically sinks.

As I mentioned, I repeatedly refused the call. After I heard the call in the shower that morning, it would be another nine years before I would fully answer the call, enter my new world by getting divorced, being let go from my job of 16 years, and starting my own business. Now, that's a lot of metaphorical death. But those old patterns needed to go so I could heal and rise like a phoenix and claim my true authentic life.

Stage Four: Meeting with The Mentor

The last stage in the preparation phase is Stage Four: Meeting with The Mentor. Before the hero has enough courage and skill to travel on his or her journey, they must first come across a seasoned traveler who gives them training, equipment or advice that will help on the journey. Or, one might reach within to a source of courage and wisdom. We've all had mentors in one form or another. They are the people we meet who inspire us and give us wisdom that helps us take that step forward. Good mentors don't have to be wise old grey haired guys; they just need to be a little further down the road to help guide you to the answers within. Mentors most always appear just as you're about to leave the ordinary world and enter the unknown special world. Mentors also know what the hero desires and what they need. While on their own journey's, they have reflected on their successes and failures, which allows them to respect the stage the apprentice is on and why they need to be there.

If the hero's commitment and competence are proven, the mentor may reward them with a special gift. This gift could be a map of the special world, an antidote to poison, or the key to a vault, or some other special magic needed for a successful quest. In many myths, the hero must pass a test to earn the gift. Great mentors possess the magic to influence their heroes in ways that are unique and with lifetime results. Mentors are legitimate shortcuts to the treasure of your Hero's Journey.

The classic mentor is depicted in the 1950 Disney movie, *Cinderella*, played by Ilene Woods, where her fairy godmother, played by Verna Felton, not only fashions a beautiful ballroom gown and a pumpkin shaped carriage, but of course, the glass slippers. And don't forget those cute little mice that became horses to draw her carriage. We can all come up with plenty of classic mentors from contemporary movies. Dorthy collected mentors along the yellow brick road to her ultimate mentor - the wizard. In *the Lord of The Rings*, the mighty wizard Gandalf mentored Frodo and the grand teacher and wizard professor, Dumbledore, mentored Harry Potter. But the most well-known mentor is the little green Jedi known as Yoda. Even though he is small, bald, has big hairy ears and talks funny, he commands great respect. The way Yoda speaks forces us to pay attention and listen to his advice. When Luke says he can't believe it, Yoda's response is "That is why you fail."

Through the years, I've hired many therapists and coaches to help me move through the times in my life when I was stuck, or to help boost my businesses. But I've also gleaned a great deal of wisdom from books or seminars I've attended to aid me on my journeys, including the late great Wayne Dyer. I remember watching him on PBS talking about connecting with our source for inspiration and guidance.

I also found Tony Robbins – now considered the father of life coaching – early in his career as a life coach. I remember attending his seminars and listening to his cassette tapes on my lunch break in my car on cold winter days. Dr. Alex Loyd, Dr. Joe Dispenza, Ken Page and Carol Pearson have also had a large impact on how I ultimately healed myself and began living my authentic life. Without mentors to teach and guide me, I would never have had the awareness to prepare for my journey.

Before I leave this topic of mentors, I would be remiss if I didn't plug my current profession of life coaching. Highly successful people know they didn't make it to the top by themselves. They all had coaches and mentors, but don't believe for a second that coaches and mentors are just for big shots. Hundreds of thousands of people participate in this time-honored tradition. No matter where you came from or where you are right now, you can also benefit from a good coach or mentor.

Let the Soul Journey Begin

From our ordinary world, we have heard, refused and finally answered the call and gathered mentors. We have identified that our Ego has developed and has prepared us for the next phase of the Hero's Journey.

Now that we are prepared, the next phase is to venture into the unknown and find our Soul. The Ego sometimes gets a bad rap as being one of the main roadblocks to finding our Soul. In contrast, it's the ability of the Ego to create and maintain our boundaries. When the Ego is properly developed, it can become the container for the Soul. It becomes a safe place for the Soul to connect with our spiritual vision.

This explains why we sometimes refuse the call for so long. We aren't ready yet, the Ego has not learned its lessons yet. The Ego needs to move through its healthy stages and be a place for the Soul to rest and feel comfortable enough for us to have the courage to take our journeys. Sadly, though, most Egos remain primitive and stuck, which does not allow the Soul to flourish and come to life.

One of the problems is that the ego sometimes gets out of control and highjacks the psyche, an entity that was never meant to lead. The ego is meant to be in the service of the soul and self. A healthy ego plays the intermediary for the whole self, while not thinking it is the whole self.

One of the ways you might recognize that you're not ready for the journey is when you find yourself continuously doing things so others will like you or think you are okay. Other signs you are not prepared include being unable to delegate, and feeling you must run everything by yourself, being afraid to say what you think because someone might get angry, or be afraid to leave a relationship or a job for fear that you can't make it on your own. Or you may realize that you are taking care of everyone in your family or office except yourself. None of these issues indicate character flaws or insurmountable obstacles. They merely indicate that you haven't fully completed the developmental tasks of learning to trust in yourself and to stand up for yourself (autonomy). Therefore, the preparation for the journey almost always starts with the Ego. Most of us have work to do to prepare for the deeper and more demanding elements of the journey. Remember that a well-balanced ego is not being egotistical or selfish. You will still care about others, but you must trust yourself to take care of yourself, and handle authority in yourself and others.

The simplest way to deal with the underdeveloped Ego's fear of change is to observe it with detachment. Before we can take our Hero's Journey, the ego needs to say yes and come along because it is the practical down to earth part that sees to it that our journeys do not spin our lives out of control.

One of the most powerful experiences I have ever had on my Hero's Journey was the first time I could detach from my Ego. A few years after my divorce, I was having a particularly hard time accepting a very difficult relationship breakup. I remember feeling this surge of rage come over me and not knowing how to deal with it. I decided I needed to burn off some energy, so I got on my bike and tore down the road. I pedaled harder than I had in years and was exhausted and sweaty and tired. I pulled my bike to the side of the trail to rest, when suddenly, I had this vision of a tiny little man throwing a tantrum, screaming and yelling and being an extreme fool. I instantly identified this as my Ego. I saw this crazy Ego off to the side of me which revealed a pure white area in my chest that I also instantly identified as my Soul. I had, for the first time ever, detached my Ego from my Soul and could see that my Soul was pure white and glowing and innocent and calm. I began to connect with my glowing Soul and my heart rate came down. I felt the most at peace in that moment than I had in a long, long time.

Being able to detach and see my ego as separate from me was key. It gave me a sense of freedom that I had been searching for. For the first time, I could deeply feel that I was no longer trapped by my Ego's rigid dependency on maintaining control and needing to please everyone. One of the areas where my Ego was undeveloped was in not trusting myself. I felt I always had to become someone I wasn't to please people. Detaching my ego and seeing my beautiful soul, freed me to love my soul, and ultimately, myself.

EXERCISE 1
YOUR LIFE TIMELINE

Complete a timeline of your life up until now. List the most significant events. This isn't a detailed list of your whole life, but it will give you a good idea of where you were in the 12 stages of the hero's journey exercise below.

Example Timeline

Year	Life Event
1962	Born in Hzelena Montana
1980	Graduated from Flathead High school
1986	Graduated from University Of Montana with a psychology degree
1987	Packed up my Honda Civic and drove across the country to start my life in Washington D.C.
1987	Got my first real job at Tymnet - Living in Northern Virginia
1989	Got married
...	...

Your Turn:

Year	Life Event

J. SCOTT MACMILLAN

EXERCISE 2
PREPARATION PHASE

Re-read the first 4 stages of the preparation phase of the Hero's Journey. Then place your life events into each stage. Make sure to identify not only what was going on in your life at this time but what the significance of this time or your life meant to you.

Don't worry if you can't identify a part of your life that doesn't fit into a particular stage. You can skip it or come back to it later.

Decide as early in the process as you can, if you are going to list out your entire life until now into one big Hero's Journey or you think you may have had more than one already. Remember that you can have multiple events in your life that may be in one stage, for example you may have had many calls to adventure but refused the call many times before actually crossing the threshold. I find it helpful to try and fit your entire life so far into one hero's journey. You may, and usually will, find that you are in the middle of your hero's journey with a few stages yet to move through.

The following questions will help you determine what preparation stage you need help with or what events should fit into a certain stage.

- What calls for change are presenting themselves to you right now?
- Are there calls from your past that you have ignored or refused? Do they still call out to you?
- What stories are you telling yourself? Are they true or simply comforting?

- Whom did you look to for direction when you were growing up?
- Are there others who acted directly or indirectly as teachers or coaches?
- Would life be different if you hadn't met these people?
- How could your life be different if you had a coach or mentor?

Stage One: The Ordinary World

- Try to remember a time in your life when you were living your life and seemingly things were fine but you felt a small inkling that something wasn't quite right and there was something more out there for you.
- Detail the date and time in your life and describe what was going on in your life at this time.

Example:

I was living in suburbia with my 2 kids and a wife. I was working my ass off to get ahead and make a good life for my family. I wasn't exercising or eating a good diet and I was becoming miserable. I began to think something in my life had to change...

Your Turn:

_____

_____

_____

Stage Two: Call to Adventure

- Now that you have established your ordinary world, follow through your timeline to when something happened in your life that woke you up and got your attention. This can be a hardship like a job loss, divorce, loss of a loved one, or it can be something that you just woke up one day and knew you had to make a change in your life.

Example:

I was in the shower when I heard a voice say "This is not the way to live your life, you must be doing something wrong."...

Your Turn:

_____

_____

_____

Stage Three: Refusal of the Call

- List the time in your life where you heard the call to adventure but were too afraid or confused to follow through and make a change in your life.

Example:

I repeatedly refused the call. After I heard the call in the shower that morning it would be another nine years before I would fully answer the call, enter my new world by getting a divorce, being let go from my job of 16 years and starting my own business...

Your Turn:

_____

_____

_____

Stage Four: Meeting with the Mentor

- Who has been a mentor to you in your life? These can be people who you admired or learned from either before your call to adventure or after. As you progress through your journey you may lean on these mentors heavily or acquire new ones.

Example:

Through the years I've hired many therapists and coaches to help me move through the stuck times in life or to help boost my businesses. But I've also gleaned a great deal of wisdom from books or seminars that I've attended to aid me on my journey...

Your Turn:

_____

_____

_____

Is your Ego prepared for the journey?

Now that you have created your preparation phase stages answer the following questions to help you decide if your Ego has progressed in a healthy developmental way. Don't be critical if you still need work in this area, most of us do.

- Do you find yourself continuously doing things so others will like you or think you are okay?
- Do you have a hard time delegating? Do you feel you must run everything by yourself?
- Do you have a hard time accepting other peoples wishes or truths even if they conflict with yours?

- Are you afraid to say what you think because someone might get angry or are you afraid to leave a relationship or a job for fear that you can't make it on your own?
- Do you have a hard time accepting constructive criticism?
- Are you taking care of everyone in your family or office except yourself?

These answers should allow you to pinpoint areas that you may need to continue to work on before or as you move into the journey and return phases. They may also show you areas that you might want to change or add to your above stages.

CHAPTER 4
PHASE II - JOURNEY OF THE SOUL - FOLLOW YOUR BLISS

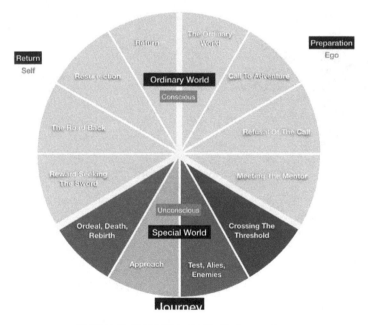

THE HERO'S JOURNEY JOURNEY MAP

In the Journey phase we finally step across the threshold into the Special World and start looking at our subconscious mind. The journey requires us to see the truth of the Soul, which doesn't necessarily make sense to the rational ego, but it's what makes us feel alive and real by journeying into the mysteries of life where we learn about life, death, intimacy, sex, passion, mystery, spirit and the things the Soul craves. Without the Soul, we feel like machines just going through the motions. Sometimes we ignore the experiences of the journey because we are so out of touch with our Souls that we are unaffected and untransformed--we have our blinders on. But make no mistake, it's never too late to cross the threshold and take our Hero's Journey. The only downfall for failing to take the Soul's journey is the ever-present sense of emptiness and meaninglessness--which is punishment enough.

Once we answer the call and cross the threshold, we step into the Soul's inner world. This is our soul's initiation process. It shakes up our way of seeing the world and requires that we connect with our deeper wisdom to understand what is happening. As you will see in the following stages, initiation may in some ways be painful as you experience suffering, confusion and loss, but it is, of course, this initiation that finally allows for the birth of the new self. This phase is also about what Campbell called "following your bliss." As your journey progresses, the essence of the Hero's Journey is in finding and following that bliss--your life's purpose and your big why.

> "Let yourself be silently drawn by the strange pull of
> what you really love. It will not lead you astray."
>
> ~ Rumi

In the journey phase of the soul, you may be asking questions like "What is my true purpose in life?" "What changes must I make?" "How can I best use my gifts and talents?". "What can I believe in?"

This is the time to examine your life and ask the tough questions. If you are in charge of your life, you must ask questions, challenge the status quo, and take responsibility for who you are, and the person you want to become.

Knowing yourself well prepares you when life in the journey phase presents sharp turns and rocky roads. This will help you in not being derailed by irrelevant chaos and noise. You'll know what you value, what's important, and why. This also allows you to make timely decisions, enhance your well-being and make the world a better place.

Recognizing your passions and landing on your purpose is where your power lies. Unfortunately, your purpose won't flash before your eyes in a "the future is so bright" moment. It's usually a slow burn that ignites a knowing and peacefulness that you understand your purpose and have figured out your big why. It's during the tests and trials of this phase that will help forge your values, beliefs and ultimately lead to your purpose.

Normal everyday activities like taking care of your family or being a good person are not your specific purpose. Of course, these are worthy activities, but they could apply to just about anyone. You need to uncover what your specific purpose is. Find where your power lies and what is unique about you that stands out, and makes a difference in other people's lives. What is it that you do better than most people? Take time to get quiet, journal and contemplate this worthwhile endeavor and I promise you will find your purpose. There are some great exercises later in the book that will help you identify your purpose.

On some level, you know you are a hero. When you find your purpose, it's like finding your superhero powers. What are your superpowers? You might not know until you fight some internal battles.

Don't get me wrong, finding your bliss and purpose is hard. It's through the battles that you'll find the answers to the burning questions you asked above. However, once you find it, it won't be all smooth sailing as doubts and fears of failure will creep up on you. But, having a purpose allows you to focus on your future and choose your battles wisely.

When you find your purpose, life flows effortlessly, you're in your power zone and you find it all exhilarating and fulfilling. Chances are, you will be drawn to helping others thrive. It's a win-win. Often, purpose and passion can be very similar and almost seem to be one. Purpose tends to be the reason you're on your Hero's Journey (The Why), while passion lights your way. Follow your passions vigorously and you'll eventually find purpose and the real Hero's Journey treasure.

Stage Five: Crossing the Threshold

In stories and movies, this is the end of act one. The hero commits to leaving the ordinary world and enters a new region or condition with unfamiliar rules and values. Crossing the threshold is when we finally answer the call and step out into the unknown. It's the scariest thing we've ever had to face but it's our time and we take that leap.

According to Campbell, once we hear the call and are willing to take on the challenges of that newly awakened life, we begin to feel a powerfulness that comes over us. We wake up seeing that we are the hero of our own lives and are tired of being the victim. Campbell also talks about a metaphorical death where something dies, so something else can live. And in every Hero's Journey, there is some death moment where something old must go and something new must stay.

In myth, when someone dies, it doesn't mean the end of a biological life. It's an indication that change is taking place. Without death, there is no transformation. The key to recognizing death is that it's just one old pattern that has played itself out and is of no use to us anymore. Which, like the phoenix, rises and gives way to some new form that has new intrinsic meaning and makes your life even bigger and better.

In the classic 1978 movie, *Superman*, directed by Richard Donner and starring Christopher Reeve, we are introduced to a young boy who has just crash-landed in a wheat field in Kansas. Young Clark, originally from the planet Krypton, has grown up hiding his superpowers from everyone because his adopted parents were afraid he would be taken from them if anyone knew what he could do. Growing up, it was sometimes hard for Clark to conceal his powers, and thus, his schoolmates would tease him.

One day, near his 18th birthday, Clark felt mysteriously called to the barn to find an emerald crystal that his biological father Jor-El, played by Marlon Brando, had created for him many thousands of years ago to learn about his heritage and reason for being sent to earth.

Crossing the threshold for our hero Clark was knowing he had to leave his widowed mother and find his true calling. He took the crystal and headed to the northern tundra where he planted the crystal in the ice, which created the Fortress of Solitude. He spent the next 12 earth years in the ice fortress learning from his father about his origin and mission. When he emerges from the fortress, he was transformed into Superman and set off on his journey.

My initial crossing the threshold moment came after I said to hell with all the doctors and physical therapists. At this point, I wasn't sure what to do other than try to chill out. For someone who had been anxious, stressed out and in pain for a long time, this proved to be a lot harder than it sounded. As I mentioned before, I started to take Tai Chi and yoga classes, and started reading on how to reduce stress. It was very slow-going and I vacillated between answering the call and refusing the call. I finally entered my new world by getting a divorce, being let go from my job of 16 years and starting my own business. All in one year! Now, that's a lot of metaphorical death. But those parts needed to go so I could find the parts that could stay and grow and be healthy, both physically and mentally.

Stage Six: Tests, Allies and Enemies

Once we finally get the courage to jump, the hero is tested, finds allies and learns the rules of the special world. The hero needs to discover who can be trusted, a sidekick may join, or an entire hero team can be forged. It's unknown because we have entered a place where we have always been too afraid to go. The hero must prepare for the greater ordeals to come and needs this stage to test skills and powers, or perhaps seek further training from the mentor. This initiation into the special world also tests the hero's commitment to the journey, and questions whether they can succeed.

Like all mythological heroes, Hercules and Achilles received their share of great strength and skills, while facing increasingly difficult challenges. This isn't so different in our lives as we are constantly bettering our skills and becoming stronger with each new challenge. We are truly the heroes of our lives.

In this stage, friends and allies will be drawn to your aid but allies must be earned. It's important to attract as many quality allies as we can to support us through the journey of the Soul.

In the 1993 movie, *Schindler's List*, Oskar Schindler, played by Liam Neeson, was a classic hero who aligned himself with Jewish allies to help him rebuild an old Polish factory to make pots and pans to sell to the German army. His main ally was Itzhak Stern, played by Ben Kingsley, a Jewish accountant who Schindler hired as his right-hand man to recruit Jewish laborers and run his business. The Jewish workers were also his allies as they worked hard so the factory would seem valuable to the Nazi's. They kept the factory open and continued to use Jewish workers, who were given a haven if they worked in Schindler's factory.

Schindler's tests came in keeping the factory open, and by extension, keeping his workers out of the death camps. On many occasions, Schindler would give his personal items to his workers to use as trade currency. Clearly he had a conscience and did what he could to save as many Jewish people as possible. In the end, Schindler created a list of over 800 Jewish workers that he paid to Commandant Goeth in exchange for moving them to Hungary, where they would eventually escape and be set free.

As for the enemy? It was the Nazi army machine itself and the evil Commandant Amon Goeth, played by Ralph Fiennes. He was pure evil as he would leisurely gun down Jewish workers as they walked down the streets.

After my divorce, I started a new career as a professional portrait photographer. Now that all my old familiar friends from the marriage and my work were gone, I had to meet new friends and forge allies. I met a particularly interesting woman and business coach in the office where my new photography studio was located. I hired her to consult me in business, she treated me like we were long lost friends. She was very professional, but had very positive energy and was extremely nice. To be honest, at first, I thought she was interested in me as more than just a client. Then one day, I saw her interacting with other people in the office and realized that was how she treated everyone. I asked her why she was so friendly and she said she just treats everyone she meets like she knows them already, and her positive energy and enthusiasm just comes out. She eventually became one of my trusted friends and allies as we created the first one of a kind (as we knew it) energy club. We would go from place to place and try to find like-minded positive energy nuts and recruit them into our club. Of course, our meetings were always held in bars, but this eventually turned into a business for her, wherein I was the official photographer. Meeting her and starting the energy club was my first initiation into understanding the power of a positive attitude, appreciating good energy, spreading the love wherever you go, and surrounding yourself with positive people. This was a powerful first education into how strong friend relationships are one key to a happy and healthy life.

My photography business morphed into a video and internet marketing consulting business and I was working out of coffee shops, and meeting new and interesting people. I found kindred souls and fellow entrepreneurs and formed strong friendships that have stayed with me to this day. One thing I learned during this time was how the Universe/ God/Creator is always supporting you if you just settle the mind and let the innate intelligence come through and work its magic. The relationships I was forming in this new period of my life would become crucial in the final painful stages of my journey. This time in my life wasn't without tests and trials though. I had worked in the corporate world all my adult life and was not nearly ready for entrepreneurship. Corporate life is completely different than being an entrepreneur and I struggled to keep up with honing my technical skills, marketing my business and dealing with all the new tax and insurance issues unique to entrepreneurs. Thankfully, I had befriended other entrepreneurs and we helped each other through the struggles.

Stage Seven: The Approach

The call has been answered and the hero and new found allies prepare for the major challenge in the special world. We know what must be done and so we prepare for it. Meetings are held, preparations are made and practice sessions commence.

The 2001 movie, *Ocean's Eleven*, the entire movie was about The Approach. Director Stephen Soderbergh set out to remake the 1960 rat pack version of this movie. It starred an ensemble cast including George Clooney Brad Pitt, Matt Damon and Julia Roberts.

Immediately after Danny Ocean, played by George Clooney, gets out of jail, he plots to rob three Las Vegas casinos at once. He rallies his gang (allies) together and begins to plan for the heist.

The movie unfolds in a fun way, wherein we learn of the plan by watching it unfold in real time. Of course, our hero, Danny, gets the money and the girl at the end.

As my consulting business was taking off, I started to focus on my body and began eating healthier and exercising more. I even went on a grain-free diet and lost 40 pounds. I dated on and off, but found I was very rusty after 19 years of marriage, and therefore didn't have much success in those early years. I started to devour my mentor's content and started practicing Chi Gong, meditation and mindfulness. As you may know, meditation is not easy at first. It takes commitment to keep doing it, despite your mind going crazy with every miscellaneous thought it can find. As I stuck with it, I began to see a gradual change in my awareness and presence. I learned about mindfulness, and it became my quest to live a mindful life. This is where I started to look inside for answers and understand how my unconscious was primarily ruling my life.

Stage Eight: The Ordeal

Near the middle of the story, the hero enters a central space in the Special World where they confront death or face their greatest fear. Out of the moment of death comes a new life, but the journey often teeters on the brink of failure. This is where we face our personal demons and battle our fears. It's scary and hard and we may feel like we've been defeated for a while. But out of defeat comes victory. Remember, this is YOUR inner journey and you are in control. Things you feared in the past are just unknowns. If you seek to understand them, you are on the path to your treasure.

Unfortunately, you can't prepare for what your exact ordeal will be. You will probably have to take a leap of faith. This is where most refuse the call and back away. Leaping into the unknown takes courage and it will take you way out of your comfort zone. To overcome the fear, the hero relies on skills and training gathered from earlier stages of the journey. We must metaphorically cut off pieces of ourselves that are holding us back from being our hero.

The hero must sacrifice and die to be re-born. Something must be given up, such as an old habit, or outdated belief--we are coming to terms with our shortcomings. The ordeal is the turning point to where everything after is changed and the hero can never go back.

If you've ever heard of the dark night of the soul, it's a term used to describe the dismantling of a perceived meaning of life. It's when we give up our preconceived notions of who we are and how we behave in life that triggers a major reset. This metaphorical rebooting can take days, weeks or months, and living through it can be the scariest thing you have ever experienced. Unfortunately, the only way out is through. You must accept it, trust it and walk through it. If you back away, it will grow stronger. For the hero, this is the confrontation of the shadow self and the biggest casualty will likely be the ego. Our greatest fear is that we won't be able to live without it--and we're right. Only through the ego's death can we experience the resurrection that empowers us to fulfill our destiny

At this stage, we are becoming aware that major change is taking place. Everything that has transpired during the journey comes to a head at the ordeal, and everything after it is about the return home. The death of the ego's stronghold opens a space for us to experience a rebirth and become the real hero of our life.

In one of my favorite movie scenes of all time, Luke Skywalker in *Star Wars: The Empire Strikes Back*, must face his greatest fear by entering the dark cave on the planet Dagobah as instructed by the Jedi Master, Yoda. As he enters the dark and dreary cave, he is confronted with snakes and creatures. He ignites his lightsaber to see better and we hear the familiar sound of Darth Vader's breathing. They face-off in a lightsaber battle where Luke finally chops off Darth Vader's head. As it falls to the ground, Luke sees that underneath the mask is his image. Luke has just faced, and metaphorically defeated, his greatest fear--that he would turn out to be evil like his father, Darth Vader.

In my experience, this stage was very long and painful. I have identified two parts of my life where I faced uphill battles and have named these my dark days. After my life changed dramatically because of my divorce, losing my job and starting my own business, things were slowly looking up. I was enjoying my new freedom and was excited about my new business. I poured my heart and soul into it, seven days a week. Unfortunately, I became lonely and frustrated with the slow growth of the business, and I started drinking a lot. It came on so slow because I had never been a big drinker. I didn't drink at all while raising my kids, but I slowly built up a tolerance and was soon drinking every night with dinner, and getting drunk at least one night a week. I started to put myself in dangerous situations by hanging out with a bad crowd. One night, I found myself at a Denny's in a part of the city I'd never been before, with armed guards at the entrance, and hanging out with people I didn't know, and in normal circumstances, would never be around. I was very lucky to find myself home in bed the next morning, but didn't know exactly how I got there. I wish I could say this was when I hit bottom, but it wasn't. I would continue to drink and gamble for another two years, until I met another lost soul who needed someone as badly as I did. That's when I a women with whom I would have an on and off relationship for the next three years. At first, we were both lost souls trying to mask our loneliness and pain with drinking. Eventually, in our time together, we healed each other a bit and were both able to curb our drinking considerably. The next phase of my ordeal came out of nowhere, like they usually do. I remember it was in the middle of a long winter and I was just down in the dumps. My girlfriend couldn't understand why I was so grumpy and never wanted to go out. I couldn't understand myself. One winter day, I noticed a weird lump under my arm but was sure it was nothing because I was not experiencing any pain or symptoms. Finally, after ignoring it for three months, I decided to have my doctor check it out. She didn't seem too concerned but thought I should get a biopsy just in case. That's not what you want to hear, but I was still optimistic they would find a clogged duct or something, and after some medication I'd be fine.

I waited over a week for the results and kept calling my doctor to see if there was any news, but she didn't know why it was taking so long. Once again, that's not good for anyone's stress level. I finally got the call everyone dreads. "Scott, you have cancer and the reason it took so long is that you have a rare form of lymphoma." Wham! The Universe/

God/Creator just knocked me on my ass again. Okay, so that's not good, I thought. But before I could get too caught up in my own grief and terror, I realized that my poor kids were now going to have both their parents in chemo at the same time, and could lose us both. Yep, my ex-wife had breast cancer and had just started her chemo sessions. It tore me up. It was harder to tell them this than it was to tell them we were getting divorced five years earlier.

This was no ordinary world. It was a crazy, scary new world filled with chemo, hair loss, radiation and fear. Thank God I had already crossed the threshold, entered my Hero's Journey and was preparing. Interestingly, about a month before I was diagnosed, I had found a new mentor named Master Lee, a renowned Chi Gong and energy healer. I had bought one of his energy healing audio classes and had been practicing daily energy healing sessions. I'm convinced that one of the reasons my chemo and radiation therapy was relatively painless and easy was because I had been practicing the daily energy exercises. Although I was lucky to catch my cancer at stage one, cancer therapy these days has come a long way, and although I lost my hair and was weak at times, I was able to carry on my work and most of my daily activities during treatment.

After my chemo, I needed to have an intense daily shot of radiation for 30 days straight. My girlfriend was a saint and was with me through the entire crazy, scary ordeal--from diagnosis through chemo treatments. We hadn't been dating that long, and I asked her to leave and told her to go on with her life after I was diagnosed, but she stayed with me and took care of me. She even shaved my head once my hair started falling out. She was my rock and I will never forget the amazing kindness and care she provided me during that time. However, it put stress on our relationship. I was just not able to be a good boyfriend as I had to focus all my attention on healing my body. After chemo, I negotiated to have my radiation back in my hometown in Montana. By luck, the director of the radiation department in Montana used to work at the radiation department of the hospital where I was having my treatments in Kansas. So, I was able to stay with my parents who lived two blocks from the radiation department in Montana, and walk to my daily treatments. The fresh mountain air, beautiful scenery and the care and love of my parents were just what I needed to heal and figure out what my next move was going to be in life.

The take-away after finishing my treatment and being cancer-free at the end of that year, was realizing how being on my journey and being aware and mindful helped with my relatively easy cancer bout. You would think that having cancer and going through treatment would be the worst thing that could happen to someone. But in my case, I realized that my first health crises with my stomach and back, and subsequently climbing out of it prepared me for dealing with cancer. Once I knew we caught it at stage one, I just knew everything was going to be alright. I just tried to be as happy and positive as I could. I chatted up every nurse, doctor and hospital food handler I could find. I feel that my positive attitude helped me cope with my life-threatening situation.

Luckily for me, I had my own consulting business and could cut way back on my hours as I healed and tried to figure out what I wanted to do with this next stage of my life. At that time, I was 52, and even though I had battled through my ordeal and claimed victory by beating cancer, I wasn't sure what path lay ahead of me. I thought about moving back to Montana full-time and settling down in my hometown and living the simple life. In the end, I decided I wasn't ready to move back to Montana, so I came back to Kansas and started up my consulting business again.

JOURNEY EXERCISE 3

Stage Five: Crossing the Threshold

- Review your timeline and find the time in your life where you finally said enough with this old way of thinking or living and actually made a change in your life. You were finally able to move out of your comfort zone and start something new or end something that needed ending and it changed your life in a new direction.
- If you can't think of a time when you feel you've crossed the threshold, then maybe you are still refusing the call or still in your ordinary life. That's okay, try and imagine a future timeline for your hero's journey and use it as a catalyst to move forward in your life.

Example:

My initial crossing the threshold came after I said to hell with all the doctors and physical therapists. At this point I wasn't sure what to do other than try to chill out...

Your Turn:

_____

_____

_____

Stage Six: Tests, Allies, and Enemies

- Now that you've crossed the threshold and living in the new unfamiliar special world, identify any trials and tribulations you went through as you moved through this new and unfamiliar territory.
- List friends and allies that appeared during this time that helped you get through these times. Also list or describe any enemies that you needed to face down. Enemies can also be difficult situations that you had to overcome.

Example:

After my divorce I started a new career as a professional portrait photographer. Now that all my old familiar friends from the marriage and my work were gone, I had to forge out and meet new friends and allies...

Your Turn:

_____

_____

_____

Stage Seven: The Approach

- Define a time in your life when you went into planning or strengthening or learning mode. This is a time in your life where you were in the thick of life. You are living in the new world and preparing to grow stronger physically, emotionally or both. You may not have known it at the time but you were preparing for even harder times ahead.
- This can be a very good time in your life when you felt like you were alive because you were moving forward.

As my consulting business was taking off I started to focus on my body and I began eating healthier and exercising more. I even went on a grain free diet and lost 40 pounds...

Your Turn:

_____

_____

_____

Stage Eight: The Ordeal

- Describe a time in your life where you had to face the scariest thing you've ever had to. Detail what it was, what you went through and the insights it brought.
- For some of us, there is more than one ordeal to identify. Just pick one at this time that fits with your timeline and hero's journey so far. There are other times in your journey where you will undergo trials and tribulations and have to face dragons and ogre's and you can list them there.

Example:

This stage for me was very long and painful. I have identified two parts of my life where I faced uphill battles and have named these my dark days...

Your Turn:

_____

_____

_____

Stage Nine: The Reward

- Identify a time in your life when you crossed the threshold, faced hardships (dragons) that you overcame and claimed victory. Be aware though, that there will be at least one more challenge to face on your journey home with the reward.

Example:

In October of the year I was diagnosed, I was declared cancer-free. I had conquered my fearful ordeal and won the battle with cancer. I was back on track living my life and consulting in Kansas...

Your Turn:

_____

_____

_____

Is your Soul prepared for the Return?

Now that you have completed the Journey phase, ask the following questions of yourself gently. As you build momentum, you can allow your fantasies to soar. Remember times when you felt satisfied or curious or content and allowed yourself to be fully present with all the sensations and images that fed your desires. Repeat each question until you have exhausted your answer: For example "I like _____ "Another thing I like is _____. Don't edit or critique your answers. Answer each question with the first words that pop into your head.

- I like
- I feel satisfied when
- I fully enjoy
- I want to do more

- I am happy when I
- What dreams do I have, day or night, that reveal my purpose?
- I feel fulfilled when I
- I feel curious about
- If I could change anything in my life I would change
- In my wildest fantasies, I have always wanted to
- List your gifts, talents and strengths
- What are my hidden gifts and talents?
- Now, review your list and decide which of these you can pass on to others
- Of all your gifts, talents and strengths, which is your best? What makes you stand out?
- What is your superpower?
- Are you willing to give up the life you've planned so you can have the life that is waiting for you?
- Where in your life are you playing defense? What would it look like to play some offense?
- Name one thing that you will do today that scares you.

These answers should allow you to pinpoint areas that you may need to continue to work on before you can move into the return phase and if you want to change any of your above Journey stages.

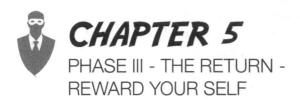

CHAPTER 5
PHASE III - THE RETURN -
REWARD YOUR SELF

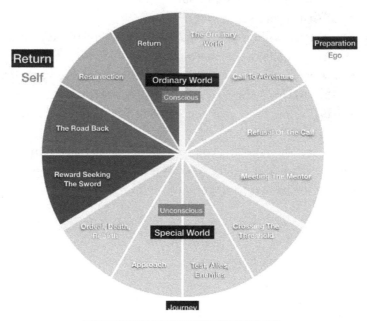

THE HERO'S JOURNEY RETURN MAP

In the final phase called the Journey, we explore the Self, which is an expression of wholeness and the endpoint in the process. The journey has been completed, the treasure gained, and the kingdom – one's life – has been transformed. Hitting the reset button all seems worth it now that we're past the ordeal. The Self is the entry point into a whole new way of living; moving us out of "life as a struggle" and into abundance. We know the journey is ending when we realize the fruits of the ordeal by finding our bliss--our authentic true self and purpose. We start acting on our new-found thoughts and ideas and begin our way back to tell our story. Being conscious is to wake up and take a new kind of responsibility for our lives and be true and authentic to ourselves, and be constructive members of the human race. We are finally able to express ourselves in the world. But no integration of consciousness lasts forever, and sooner or later that consciousness will split and the journey will begin again.

We have been through the preparation and journey phases, and we now enter the final phase of self-renewal. The transition from change to renewal is life-changing.

On the surface, the goal of the outward journey is a visible achievement in reaching the destination or winning the battle. The purpose of the inner journey is internal fulfillment and self-actualization. While the inciting incident, the call to adventure, triggers the outward quest, it is an incessant call from within that provokes heroes to achieve their destiny. In the classic definition, a hero is someone who gives their life to something bigger than themselves. The journey is of initiation--of awakening an inner power of spiritual knowing. Facing both external and internal obstacles, the hero confronts fears, as well as external challenges to ensure survival. Conquering the forces rallied against them, heroes emerge as their authentic selves--victorious and empowered.

Bringing unconscious limiting beliefs into the light of consciousness is great, but once we realize we're unconscious, we must identify the culprits. Pushing through the rest of the block requires us to be accountable for our commitments. When we say were' going to do something and are true to our word, motivation improves and our commitment gets stronger. We can stay on track and move forward. Accountability is the bond to our commitment to getting results.

Stage Nine: The Reward

The hero takes possession of the treasure won by taking the journey and facing death. There may be a celebration, but there is also danger of losing the treasure again.

As the hero of your journey, you took the bull by the horns and transformed misfortune into fortune. You wouldn't be the same person today without the misfortunes you have endured. Most of us will do anything to avoid misfortune, but we need not run from it as we only accomplish success through experiencing misfortunes. It's our responsibility to transform misfortune into our treasure.

Widely regarded as one of the best movies of all time, director Francis Ford Coppola brought to life Mario Puzo's novel, *The Godfather*, which debuted in 1972. The movie depicts the powerful Italian-American crime family of Don Vito Corleone, played brilliantly by Marlon Brando. The Dons youngest son, Michael, played by Al Pacino, reluctantly joins the family business after his father's death. In a full-out power grab, Michael has all the other heads of the New York mafia killed. Michael celebrates his victory by lying to his wife Kay, played by Diane Keaton, about having anything to do with his sister's husband being killed and having his men kiss his hand. He is the new Godfather now. Just as any good Hero's Journey movie, this only marks the beginning of potential danger ahead, as depicted in The Godfather II and The Godfather III.

In October of the year I was diagnosed, I was declared cancer-free. I had conquered my fearful ordeal and won the battle with cancer. I was back on track, living my life and consulting in Kansas. I had moved into a new apartment, started a new area of consulting in internet marketing and wrote my second book called "Monetize Your Message". It was a book on how to create online courses and sell them on the internet. I was happy and trying to get my strength back and wanting to get back in the dating pool again, since my hair had grown back and I had lost a few pounds. Little did I know that my next phase of the journey would entail even more pain and suffering, this time emotional, but ultimately lead to an enlightenment that would change the course of my life yet again and prepare me for my return.

Stage Ten: The Road Back

About three-fourths of the way through the story, the hero is driven to complete the adventure, leaving the Special World to bring the treasure home. Often, a chase scene signals the urgency and danger of the mission. This is a critical stage because no matter what the victory, we must complete the journey and bring back the treasure. This is where a lot of us falter; we take our eye off the ball and we fumble.

The road back is fraught with peril and no one had as many obstacles to surpass than Indiana Jones, played by Harrison Ford in the 1981 movie, *Raiders of The Lost Ark*, directed by Steven Spielberg. Most of the movie shows the perilous road back for Indiana after he finds the lost treasure of the Ark of the Covenant.

Just as he finds the Ark in an underground cavern in Cairo, the Nazi army, who also wants the Ark, traps him in the cavern and takes the Ark. Of course, a dark cave filled with snakes is no match for Indiana Jones. After he escapes the cavern, he steals a horse, finds the Nazi's caravan carrying the Ark and manages to highjack a truck and get the Ark onto a ship to transport back to the U.S.

But as we are promised in the road back, the Nazi's catch him in a submarine and steal the Ark back again. Before they present the Ark to Hitler, the Nazi's decide to open the Ark to make sure it contains the treasure inside. This turns out to be a big mistake as when they open the it spews torrents of flames that kill all the Nazi's. Indiana is unhurt by the flames because he kept his eyes shut as they opened the Ark. That's what I would have done right?, closing your eyes always works. He finally brings the treasure home where the U.S. Government confiscates the Ark for their own study.

At this stage in my life, the only chase scene I was experiencing was my dating failures and chasing my tail trying to find true love again. I tried various ways to find my soulmate--from meetups, to online dating, to hanging out in bars, with no success. I was beginning to feel discouraged that I may have dropped the ball on my journey, and that I was stuck again. After my divorce six years earlier, I figured my life would be further along. But, I was still single and living in an apartment.

Stage Eleven: The Resurrection

After the climax, the hero is severely tested once more on the threshold of home. He or she is purified by a last sacrifice – another moment of death and rebirth – but on a higher and more complete level. By the hero's action, the polarities that were in conflict at the beginning are being resolved. This is probably the most difficult stage for us. We are so close. We are happy that we've made so much progress, and we're celebrating on the road home when the most severe test yet knocks us on our ass yet again. But here's the key. At this point, we've already been through a lot, we have moved through the stages of healthy Ego development and taken our Soul journey, faced dragons and ogres and gained friends and mentors. We are as healthy and emotionally evolved as we have ever been. We've gained knowledge and power that we didn't know was possible. So, even though this is a huge test, we are ready for it. And finally, after this purifying event, those polarities that have been plaguing us most of our lives have finally been put to rest.

The Resurrection may be a physical ordeal or final showdown between the Hero and the Shadow. This battle is for much more than the Hero's life. Other lives, or an entire world, may be at stake, and the Hero must now prove that they have achieved Heroic status and willingly accept their sacrifice for the benefit of the Ordinary World. Other allies may come to the last-minute rescue to lend assistance, but in the end, the Hero must rise to the sacrifice at hand. They must deliver the final blow and accept the "magic elixir."

In the 1995 smash hit, *Toy Story*, directed by John Lasseter, our hero Woody, played by Tom Hanks, gets himself into a bit of a pickle. Because he is jealous of Andy's new toy, Buzz Lightyear, played by Tim Allen, he inadvertently knocks Buzz out of the window and Buzz lands in the backyard of the evil toy-destroying boy named Sid.

While attempting to rescue Buzz from Sid, Woody ends up in Sid's room with Buzz, and both are faced with their apparent doom. Woody's resurrection comes when he has a chance to escape on his own, but decides he can't leave Buzz behind. He convinces Sid's maimed toys to help by coming to life in front of Sid and scaring the crap out of him. Both Woody and Buzz escape and rush to catch the moving van taking Andy's family to a new house. Andy's other toys come to their rescue and help them get back to Andy's new room, where they can live their lives with Andy and his family.

This next part of my story may sound unremarkable to you, but it was significant event in my life because it was the catalyst to my growth and healing. Remember, everyone's Hero's Journey is personal, and for some, the call to adventure, the ordeal or the resurrection is a love loss. I had been dating on and off since returning to Kansas, but nothing was even remotely serious. One day, out of the blue. I met a woman who I would fall in love with and who profoundly changed the course of my life.

We dated on and off for a year but when it ended I took it pretty hard. During the painful on and off period in our relationship, I was digging deep inside to figure out why I was suffering so much. I kept telling myself that breakups happen all the time, and I asked myself why this one was so painful for me. I had many relationships come and go and was married for 19 years, but nothing came close to the suffering I was feeling after this breakup. Luckily, I was on the return home of my journey and I had accumulated mystical powers and trusted allies. My mystical power turned out to be the ability to see that the answer to my suffering was within me, not outside. It wasn't her, her friends, my friends or anyone other than something inside me that had been triggered, and some deep feeling was activated and needed to be heard. I began to read about the Buddhist approach to suffering and learned the concept of the Four Nobel Truths. They are that suffering exists and arises from attachment to desires, and ceases when attachment to desire ceases. You see, I had created a fantasy in my head about us and I became so attached to that fantasy, that the reality of the situation didn't seem to matter. When I understood this, I could see that I was in love with the fantasy more than I was with her. I began to journal daily about my suffering to make sense of it. I began to see that my subconscious was being triggered.

I eventually gleaned that I had a severe case of unworthiness as a child, and this breakup somehow triggered that small unworthy child inside me like nothing else had in my life. This was also very hard to understand because I had a very wonderful and happy childhood. My parents who are still alive and married today were wonderful parents, and I grew up in a perfect little town in Montana. I basically had everything a child could want, but I also began to remember that I was a very sensitive child and it would have only taken a very small scolding or unfriendly gesture to cause me to be very negative and create a lasting subconscious limiting belief that I was unworthy. As I grew up, I felt less smart, less athletic, and less handsome than my peers. But because of my journey, I learned how to tap into this limiting belief and heal it. I also had to realize that being sensitive was a real part of me, and that I had been pushing that away most of my life. Sensitive boys were not rewarded when I was young. Again, I had wonderful parents who did the best they could, but they made sure that when I scrapped my knee, I rubbed dirt on it and got back out there. Allowing myself to finally embrace my sensitivity was very healing. I realized that I could be a sensitive but masculine man, and that this was a gift rather than a curse. It's what is attractive about me and allows people to trust and like being around me. Not everyone of course, you can't please everyone right? The problem was that even though I started to acknowledge my sensitivity, I didn't really accept it. There was still unconscious programming that believed being sensitive was not good. I eventually learned that being authentic is not just trying to love and accept yourself, it's actually being okay with yourself and to be willing to put that part out into the world with no excuses or reservations.

The opening that was created started to expand and I found there were other areas of my life that needed work. I began to examine my work life and began to figure out if I was doing what I truly loved to do, and if I was living in my bliss as Joseph Campbell would say. Part of that path came with getting out of my head and into my heart and helping people. I began to volunteer with local nonprofits and give away my time and talents to help them and others. It felt good to help others--it is one of life's most powerful healing elixir's. Just as Campbell states that part of the Resurrection is a fight for more than just the hero, I started a blog called "Be the Change You Want" that highlighted people working together to solve the nation's problems, instead of being so divisive. I also started writing for an online spiritual magazine about the Hero's Journey, and the genesis of Hero Life was born. I realized that I wanted to help others who were stuck in their lives and needed a way to understand themselves better. I wanted to help them find their true mission and live a fulfilling life. I also had a few dear friends (allies) that stood with me during my suffering and didn't try to fix me; they just listened with acknowledgment and grace.

If you are at this stage but still don't seem to know what your passion is or your gifts to the world are, try looking at your suffering. Diving deep to figure out the source of your suffering will illuminate your greatest gifts. It worked for me and I know it will work for you too.

Stage Twelve: Return with the Elixir/Treasure

Returning with the treasure is the final reward that is earned on the Hero's Journey. The Hero has been resurrected, purified and has earned the right to be accepted back into the Ordinary World and share the treasure of the journey. The true Hero returns with treasure to share with others or heal a wounded land. The treasure can be great wealth or a magic potion. It can also be love, wisdom, or simply the experience of having survived the Special World. These treasures allow us to return to our ordinary conscious world and share valuable insights and perspectives and heal others as you have healed yourself.

In the 2009 movie, *Avatar*, directed by James Cameron, we see the crippled war marine, Jake Sully, take over his dead brother's human/Na'vi hybrid called an avatar on the planet Pandora. The Na'vi who are indigenous to Pandora appear primitive, but are highly evolved. As Jake integrates with the Na'vi, he falls in love with the people and the chief's daughter, Neytiri.

A human organization called the RDA attacks the Na'vi so they can mine the profitable mineral called unobtanium. Our hero Jake defeats the most terrifying predator on Pandora, which gains him ultimate Na'vi respect, which he uses to rally all the Na'vi tribes and animals to fight and defeat the RDA. After the battle, the remaining humans are sent away and Jake finds his treasure by transferring his conscience to his Avatar and becoming a full Na'vi to live the rest of his life on Pandora.

As I mentioned, this book is in part my return. Completing my Hero's Journey opened a whole new avenue of creativity for me. During my journey, I realized I wanted to pursue helping people again through education and mindful thinking, so I wrote this book and became a life coach. I am now living in my true authenticity and pursuing my purpose. Of course, my treasure is having attained a healthier Ego, Soul and Self, as well as pursuing my purpose, but it's my deepest wish that this book will be a story I brought back that helps you realize your own Hero's Journey.

As I mentioned before, the Hero's Journey is a great framework to put your own life into. As you have seen from my story, I was able to understand a great deal about my life by understanding what part of the Hero's Journey I was on at different times in my life. We may have numerous Hero's Journeys, each one an evolution in our growth. Some trips take a short time, some take longer. Each mini-journey within the lifelong journey brings us closer to mastering our worlds. Mini journeys happen over time. Your time away at college, raising your kids, the years in a past marriage, your first career. The events in our lives have a way of segmenting themselves when we take a birds-eye view of them--unlike when we're living them. The Hero's Journey helps us reconcile the seeming randomness of our lives. By documenting our preparation, journey and return, we are granted insights to their purpose and why we needed to follow that path during that time. Looking back, we grasp the significance of life's lessons. Going forward, the Hero's Journey is a guiding metaphor for our future journeys.

Now that you've returned home, you will take on the mentor role. It comes with the territory of having mastered your life. Your gifts and talents can now be generously passed onto others, especially to those that have just received the call. You will soon be the mentor helping shape other journeyers with what you have learned. Consider it a passing of the baton.

Knowing that all heroes (and all of us are our own hero) go through very hard times but always move past them and are better off for it, is comforting. We can begin to see how our struggles strengthened us and how we are all heroes who can obtain the treasure life has to offer.

Keep in mind though, that heroes do the hard things and ask the tough questions that most people don't. Keep asking yourself if you are making a difference and contributing substance and significance.

EXERCISE 4
RETURN PHASE

Stage Ten: The Road Back

- Identify a time in your life when you crossed the threshold, faced hardships (dragons) that you overcame and claimed victory. Be aware though, that there will be at least one more challenge to face on your journey home with the reward.
- This is a critical stage because you must return home after the victory. Remember a time in your life where you had achieved victory and were on the road back home to the ordinary world. Again, you will still be tested again before reaching home.

Example:

At this stage in my life the only chase scene I was experiencing was my dating failures and my chasing my tail trying to find true love again. I was trying various ways to find my girlfriend. From meetups to online dating to hanging out in bars with no success stories...

Your Turn:

_____

_____

_____

Stage Eleven: The Resurrection

- This may be the most interesting stage in the journey. It was for me at least. Just when you think you have defeated your dragons and claimed victory on your way home, you are severely tested one more time. Think of a time in your life where after a victory you were tested or faced one more challenge that purified you with one last lesson. Remember that even though this challenge may be the most severe, you have been on your hero's journey and have gained valuable insights, skills and mentors to help you face this last challenge.

Example:

I had been dating on and off since returning to Kansas but nothing was even remotely serious until one day out of the blue I met a women who would profoundly change the course of my life...

Your Turn:

_____

_____

_____

Stage Twelve: Return with the Treasure

- You finally made it back to your ordinary world with treasure in hand. You have gained much insight and strength during your journey. Your reward is either something tangible, like a new job, a relationship, renewed health or even more likely an amazing story of survival to tell your tribe.
- List a time where you found your true authentic self and were living your life purpose.

Example:

As I mentioned, this book is in part my return. Completing my hero's journey opened a whole new avenue of creativity for me. During my journey I encountered many mentors and healers and through meditation and journaling I realized that I have always had a sense to help people through education...

Your Turn:

_____

_____

_____

Have You Found Yourself?

- What is my personal kingdom, and what are my responsibilities to myself?
- What are my responsibilities to other people?
- Write a description of your role and responsibilities in the following areas of life:
  - Family
  - Primary relationship
  - Work
  - Church or community group
- Is it your turn to give back and pay it forward?
- Are you prepared to be a mentor?

EXERCISE 5
HERO'S JOURNEY SUMMARY

Now that you have broken down your life according the stages of the Hero's Journey it's time to put it all together and draw some conclusions. You want to figure out where in your life you have been the hero that was called to adventure, where you battled your metaphorical dragons and came out the victor. You also want to know where you refused the call. See if you can figure out why you refused the call for so long before you had the courage to cross the threshold and take your journey. What finally gave you the courage to move forward? Do you still have that courage today or have you lost it some how?

Review all of your stages and put together a few paragraphs of what you have gleaned by sorting your life into stages of the Hero's Journey. If you get on a roll and find yourself writing pages and pages, by all means go for it. This can be a very cathartic and eye opening experience. I know it was for me.

In latter exercises you will be identifying your limiting stories, beliefs and behaviors. You will want to use your Hero's Journey story to help identify those.

Example:

I started my adult life full of hope and passion. I wanted to live the American dream of owning a house in the suburbs, enjoying time with my wife and watching my kids grow up. What I didn't realize is that I was predisposed to general anxiety disorder and as I pursued the dream I was piling on heaps of stress and secreting stress producing hormones into my body with no escape. Basically I was in flight or fight all the time and the human body isn't made to function that way.

My Hero's Journey started when I heard the call to adventure in the shower one morning. But unfortunately it would be over 10 years before I would accept the call and cross the threshold into the unknown world. My wake up call was getting laid off and divorced in the span of one year. The Universe knocked me on my ass.

I struggled for years in the unknown world drinking too much and feeling lonely and then getting cancer. But I rallied and healed and made a comeback by helping others and writing about my experiences in life.

After I returned from my journey and claimed victory, I took up the mantle of mentor and wrote this book and started life coaching to help people with life's challenges and helping them move forward as I did.

As this journey ends I embark on a new Hero's Journey as I build my business and foster a life time relationship with the women I love.

Your Turn:

_____

_____

_____

SECTION TWO
TRANSFORMATION

CHAPTER 6
INSIDE OUT THINKING

Now that we understand that we are the heroes of our own lives, you might be asking, okay I get it but I don't feel like a hero. As you saw from mythology and movies, heroes are made, not born. If you've identified parts of your life wherein you were a hero for moving through a difficult time and learning from it, that's amazing, right? But if you haven't identified yourself as a hero yet or know your hero skills could use some work, then there are proven ways to take that inner journey, find your bliss, supercharge your life and become a superhero.

To create lasting transformation it takes new ways of thinking. The rest of this book is about transformation into your superhero self, but to do that it's going to be necessary to think differently. The next few chapters will present you with new ways to view our experience of life and what we think is reality.

Inside Out Thinking

What makes up the human experience? Is it what we can feel, touch and taste with our senses? The inside out principles imply that mind, thought and consciousness are the fundamental sources that make up the human experience. This inside out concept had begun appearing in the literature under names, ranging from Psychology Of Mind to Heath Realization to the Three Principles. The two most influential practitioners of this concept were Richard Carlson, author of "Don't

Sweat The Small Stuff" and Syd Banks a Scottish welder who had an enlightenment experience and was transformed from an uneducated worker in a pulp mill into a world-renowned guru and teacher.

The Mind

In this theory, the mind makes up the energy that runs through all things but in this case it's not the same as the brain, although mind energy is in our physical brains. It is what allows our hearts to beat, blood to flow, and mental activity to power our brains. The mind is not specific to you, it's the simple human energy and intelligence that runs through us all. As long as you are living, the mind is an engine that allows you to have the next heartbeat, the next breath and the next thought - it literally turns on our experience of life.

Thought

We create our individual experience of reality via the vehicle of thought. Thought is the missing link between the formless world of pure potentiality and the created world of form. Without a thought, you can't have an experience. Without thought, we can't have a self or a notion of who we are. We create the understanding of ourselves via our thoughts. If you have and experience of something, it has to be in your thinking.

Thought is all around us but invisible. Without thought, there would be no separation in our world - no perception, no distinction, and no variety of experience. Thought is both the creator and substance of our beliefs and values and is the raw material of our ideas and dreams. We are aware that thought is what we think but we tend to be unaware of how much of life itself is created and maintained by thought. Much of what appears to be solid and real is actually part of the illusion of our thinking.

Consciousness

Consciousness is what brings our thinking to life and makes us aware of what we're thinking. It allows us to feel our thinking. It's kind of like the special effects department of the human system. Our thinking runs through our sensory system, giving us a super surround sound and high definition experience of our thoughts. If feels completely real and as if it's coming from something other than our thinking. But it's not. In order to feel anything, we have to be conscious. Consciousness is more powerful than the greatest Hollywood special effect team could ever be, because whatever we think, consciousness will bring to life in our body and make it feel absolutely real. The capacity to be aware and experience life is innate in human beings. It is a universal phenomenon. Our level of awareness in any given moment determines the quality of our experience.

The human mind can be seen like an old fashioned film projector. In thought, we create a picture of life and project it out on to the screen of our experience. We live in a movie of our own making.

THE MIND IS THE POWER SOURCE, THOUGHT IS THE FILM AND CONSCIOUSNESS IS THE LIGHT SOURCE. ONE HUNDRED PERCENT OF OUR EXPERIENCE IS COMING FROM THE INSIDE-OUT RATHER THAN THE OUTSIDE IN.

This concept clears up a lot of misconceptions and frustrations people have when they feel like the world is happening to them, as opposed to coming from within them. When you grasp this concept you essentially stop feeling at the mercy of things outside yourselves. Thought is just temporary energy and basically not real. It comes into the mind and then goes. While it's there it can seem very real and compelling, but if you don't do anything with it, it will pass.

While most of us understand that thought is basically what we think about, we tend to be unaware of how much of life itself is created by thought. Much of what appears to be solid and real is actually part of the illusion of our thinking. Take icebergs for example, they appear solid, but are actually made up of water. Just a small degree of fluctuation in temperature can destroy icebergs that have been around for hundreds of years. In our inner world, no matter how solid our reality may seem, it only takes a slight shift in consciousness for our entire world to change.

Therefore the phrase, "This too shall pass" takes on a whole new meaning. If you give your mind the opportunity, it will self-correct and gravitate toward a clearer state of mind. And an innate intelligence, that we all have, will come forth.

Thoughts can be seen as the mediator through which we experience life. They are actually just energy that takes a form in our head. When we are inside whatever form that thought takes, that's what we experience. It may be happy or sad, stressed, fearful or even just what you want for dinner tonight. And here is a crucial point, when the volume is turned up on a thought or held tightly, it has a larger presence on us. When we don't hold on tightly to our thinking or play it too loudly in our minds it just slides through us staying only briefly. Generally the louder and tighter our thinking gets, the more alone, frustrated and frighted we become because we feel stuck. That's why when something very traumatic happens in our lives it's harder to let go of it. The volume on that experience is turned way up. Yet when our thinking is quiet and more fluid we feel a sense of connection with people because our individual thoughts aren't so prominent and isolating, and we feel there is a flow moving life along on our behalf rather than having to personally make life happen for us.

Understanding this concept of inside out thinking allows us to have insights into the nature of the human condition and opens up a higher perspective, and deeper understanding of what's really going on. The simple truth is this: Our experience of life is created from the inside out via the principles of mind, consciousness and thought. We're living in the feeling of our thinking, not the feeling of the world.

"The world is a divine dream, suspended between the boundaries of time, space and matter." ~ Syd Banks

Transformation

With an understanding of inside out thinking then, how do we create true transformation and move into that comfortable feeling of trusting our innate wisdom?

The Hero's Journey lays out the perfect formula for creating a transformative shift in our lives. We are living in our normal day to day existence when somethings happens in our lives that changes our point of view. This new view gives us the courage to make a change in our lives. We go from inaction to action, from stuck to flowing, from miserable to happy. We stop our numbing behaviors like smoking, drinking or excessive shopping. Before long, our career takes off, relationships improve and our creative output increases. Such a transformation is not the result of intervention, but rather the effect of a shift in our level of consciousness by understanding that we are and have been the hero's of our own life. That we can handle what life dishes out to us because we have done it before and can do it again.

Remember the first time you fell in love? Suddenly the world seemed a more beautiful place. We were inspired to write poetry, draw pictures or create things that reflect the beautiful feelings we felt inside. But because we attributed those feelings to another person, we often times return to our old ways of thinking and feeling. But those feelings didn't come from outside of us, they are part of our essential selves. When we can see that fundamental truth, the shift in consciousness becomes permanent and a new way of seeing becomes available to us.

These transformative shifts are actually insights which are these wonderful 'Aha' moments when we're able to see something about ourselves, our lives, or in life itself in a whole new way. If there is anything to be done, it comes effortlessly. In these wonderful transformative moments we find a fresh new way of seeing things that we may have been feeling for a long time. We just 'get it', but not intellectually the way we might understand a concept but at an almost cellular level. An isight is really just a new thought but can change our world because you can have a fresh thought at any moment. Our thinking changes moment by moment, so the ability to have a new thought about an old situation is natural and ever present. Sometimes these thoughts seem to arise from somewhere beyond us and contain wisdom outside of our current knowledge. These are part of our natural intelligence of mind and we experience them as common sense, gut feelings or innate wisdom.

Now that we have experienced a new insight we have a decision to make. We can continue to try and control life and attempt to think, behave or change the world in our quest for happiness and well-being. This is where most people are, we'll find many companions on this path. Or we can take the path of transformation and give up our attachment to the comforting feelings of being in control. We give up the illusory safety of the known in search of the unknown. - the field of all possibility and where miracles happen.

When we can simply step into the realm of insight and be in the unknown, we can appreciate the mystery of being alive. While we don't control the timing of these perceptions each time we have one, we see life in a new and clearer way.

CHAPTER 7
QUANTUM CREATING

We've all heard the phrase, "thoughts become things," right? Do you believe it? If you do, I bet you are constantly focusing all your attention on what you want instead of always thinking about your problems right? Frankly though, most of us focus way too much on our problems and how we can solve them. To create any real and lasting change in our life, we need to find a way to overcome the years of our unconscious mind running the show. To do that, it will take a new way at looking at reality. You'll need to be open to some new interpretations of what is real and true. Stay with me, this is going to be fun.

Although the science of quantum physics and unified quantum field theory have been around for over a century and been written about by many credible scientists, the following accumulation of information that I'm about to share primarily comes from the esteemed Dr. Joe Dispenza. He has written many books on the concept of the quantum field and what he calls quantum creating. We'll touch briefly on his theories and use them as a basis for creating lasting change and becoming true heroes in our lives.

To begin, let's start with a bit of history and science. What, not up for going back to grade school? I promise this will be easy. In the 17th century, mathematician and philosopher Rene Descartes couldn't rationalize his understanding of the physical world and the mind, so he declared them separate. Thus began the realm that matter is for science and the mind is for God, which fell to religion and lasted for many years. Sir Isaac Newton, with his classical Newtonian physics movement, considered all matter to be solid. What these two giants of the scientific community basically postulated was that humanity had little to no influence on outcomes, and that reality was predetermined. Is it any wonder why humans struggle to feel that their actions or thoughts matter, let alone that freedom plays any part in life?

Quantum Physics to The Rescue

Albert Einstein's famous E=MC2 equation demonstrates that energy and matter are fundamentally related. His theory shows that matter and energy are completely interchangeable. This directly contradicted Newton and Descartes, and gave way to a new understanding of how the Universe/God/Creator works; thus, Quantum physics was born, which basically states that the most fundamental components of our world are both waves (energy) and particles (matter), and which is present at the time, depends on the observer .

The old model of the atom showed that it is mostly made up of a solid nucleus with smaller objects surrounding it. We now know that an atom is far from solid. In fact, it is 99.99999 percent energy and .00001 percent matter. The other interesting phenomenon that was discovered was that not only is the atom made of both energy and matter, but that either of those states exists only momentarily. Basically, matter is constantly appearing and disappearing. What quantum physics discovered was that the person observing the tiny particles of an atom affects the behavior of the energy and matter. Electrons exist simultaneously in an infinite array of possibilities or probabilities in an invisible field of energy. Only when an observer focuses their attention on any one electron, does it appear. In other words, a particle cannot manifest until we observe it. With this information, we can no longer consider mind and matter separate.

This is amazing news because it shows us that our mindful attention can affect change on matter and that everything in our physical reality exists as pure potential. If we can imagine it, then it already exists as a possibility in the quantum field, waiting for our mind to collapse it into reality. Just like play-doh, the energy of infinite possibilities is shaped by our consciousness.

Creating Change

With this new view of matter and the world, you can begin to see how we can affect lasting change in our lives. By increasing our skills of mindful focus of our thoughts and desires, we can create and live our chosen authentic and mission-driven lives and become the heroes we were meant to be.

But how can our thoughts and feelings create change? As Dr. Dispenza points out, the quantum field (Universe/God/Creator) doesn't respond simply to vague wishes or thoughts. It only responds when the mind and body are aligned or coherent and are broadcasting the same signal. This point can't be stressed enough. You must literally feel the feelings and emotions of the person you want to become in the moment, so you create a powerful electromagnetic frequency that broadcasts into the Universe/God/Creator (field of all possibilities). If we continue with our routine of known thoughts and feelings, we will just perpetuate the same old state, which created the same old behaviors, and will create the same old reality. Therefore, if we want to change our reality, we must think, feel and act in new ways. We must be different in terms of our response to life's experiences. We need to generate a new electromagnetic signature that will match a potential reality in the Universe/God/Creator and have that potential reality pulled to us.

So, you can see that what you say to yourself does matter and will determine your fate. You see, your subconscious mind pays attention to every thought and our only control is the type of instructions we provide it. If you think your life sucks, your subconscious hears that.

You may not be aware that your negative self-talk is that big of a deal, but your subconscious takes it all in. It will attempt to give you what you want--it is very disciplined this way.

The problem is that it's not very good at deciphering moods, doubts, and fears. In fact, your subconscious mind cannot reason at all, as its only job is to obey your commands. Reasoning comes from your conscious mind only. When you tell yourself that today is going to be a bad day because that's just the way it's always been for you, your subconscious hears that and says, okay I heard you and here is your bad day. Of course, you didn't mean for it to take what you said so literally, and you probably didn't realize you just commanded your subconscious to have a bad day. Our subconscious cannot distinguish our real intent. Everything we say passes to it without going through any filters.

For example, if you were joining a new school or a new job and you said to yourself, I probably won't bond with anyone here, so I might as well just sit here by myself in the lunch or break room, your subconscious mind will do everything in its power to grant the wish of not finding a friend. We were only saying that because we didn't want our feelings to be hurt if no one talked to us. But it is undermining our ultimate desire to be liked. The subconscious doesn't mean to do this of course; it's just following the orders we gave.

When things happen to us, we attach a meaning to it and hand it over to the subconscious for safe keeping. When a similar event in our life happens, it quickly provides us with a reaction to deal with the current situation based on this historical precedent. The problem is that these stories are sometimes very old and need updating.

Once we embrace that we are the culmination of every thought we've ever had, we can begin to recognize that we have created our world and we can take responsibility for it. It also allows us to know we have the power to change our world by simply changing our thoughts. We can rewrite our story through new thoughts and feelings.

For this to this work though, you need to create a very coherent signal that is broadcast to the Universe/God/Creator. In physics, a coherent signal is made up of waves that are 'in phase', which are obviously more powerful. The same goes for your thoughts and feelings. If you were an early follower of the Law of Attraction, and were frustrated by not manifesting your dreams and wishes, it was probably due to the fact that thoughts alone don't create a coherent signal that is powerful enough. Creating a reality in the Universe/God/Creator only works when our thoughts and feelings are aligned.

To change our reality, we must also be surprised by the way these realities unfold. Dr. Dispenza warns us that we should not try to predict how our new creation will manifest. These manifestations should leave no doubt that we have created a strong electromagnetic signal with our mind/body, and that it made contact with the Universe/God/Creator and created our new reality. If you're trying to control the outcome, then you are playing the cause and effect game where you are waiting for something to happen in your outer experience before you validate it internally. So, when you are manifesting your new reality, you want to hold a clear intention of what you want, but leave the details to the unpredictable Universe/God/Creator.

Dr. Dispenza further suggests another quantum-manifesting rule that you should follow. You want to live in a state of gratitude as if you have already experienced your wanted reality. We are conditioned to believe that we need a reason to be grateful. We wait for an external reality to happen and then we are grateful that it appears in our lives. This is the old cause and effect model again. To truly be a quantum creator, we want to give thanks and feel the elevated emotions associated with a desired event before it occurs. We need to imagine this reality so completely that we begin to be in that future life in the present. We are giving thanks for something that exists as a potential in the Universe/God/Creator but has not yet happened in our reality. When we are in a state of gratitude, we transmit a signal into the field that an event has already occurred. This is more than an intellectual thought experiment.

Your body, which only understands feelings, needs to feel as though you are living in your new reality right now.

Why is it so Hard to Change?

Let's look at how the brain works as Dr. Dispenza walks us through this complicated piece of grey matter called the brain so we can better understand why it's so hard to change but also how, if we are consistent, we can begin to change who we are.

According to Dr. Dispenza, most people focus on three things in life: Their environment, their bodies, and time. We think equal to them. But to create a new you, we must think greater than the circumstances of our life, and be greater than the feelings we have memorized in our bodies and live in a new line of time. To effect change, we must have in our thoughts an idealized self (our hero model) that we can emulate, which is different from what exists today in our specific environment, body and time.

As we live our lives, the environment causes us to think and familiar networks of nerve cells reflect previous experiences that are already wired in our brain. Essentially, we automatically think in familiar ways derived from memories. If our thoughts determine our reality, and we keep thinking the same thoughts produced by the environment, then we will continue to produce the same reality day after day. Thus, our internal thoughts and feelings will match our external life, which is full of life's problems, conditions and circumstances.

We could say then, that the environment is controlling our minds because we are repeatedly reproducing the same level of thought and 'reminding' ourselves who we think we are based on our reference to the outer world. Our identity literally becomes defined by everything outside of us and we continually collapse infinite waves of probabilities of the Universe/God/Creator into events that reflect the mind and we create more of the same old same. Each morning, our senses plug us into the same reality and initiate the same stream of consciousness. All the sensory input that our brain processes from the external world, (seeing, smelling, hearing, feeling, and tasting) turns our brains on to think equal to everything familiar in our external reality. We open our eyes and we know who our children are because of our past experiences together. We associate the outer, familiar world with who we think we are, by remembering ourselves in this dimension, time and space.

Stay with me here, I know it's getting deep. Basically, we wake up in the morning and follow the same routine, go to work and do the same thing, then hurry home, do the same thing and go to bed so we can do it all over the next day. The question is, why are we secretly expecting something different to show up in our life when we think the same thoughts, perform the same actions and experience the same emotions every single day? Isn't that the definition of insanity? After some time, our brains will create a finite set of circuits that create a very specific mental signature. This signature is called our personality. As long as our minds remain the same, our lives will stay the same.

Emotions = Chemicals Which = Addiction

Did you know that every time you have a thought there is a biochemical reaction in the brain? The chemical signal is released to the body as a message of thought. When the body gets these chemical messages from the brain, it complies instantly by initiating a matching set of reactions directly in alignment with what the brain is thinking. The body immediately sends a confirming message back up to the brain that it's now feeling exactly the way the brain is thinking--we call this an emotion. Therefore, when you have loving thoughts or joyous thoughts, you produce chemicals that make you feel the emotions of love or joy. The same holds true if you have negative or fearful thoughts. In a matter of seconds, you begin to feel negative or fearful emotions. There's a synchronicity that takes place moment-by-moment between the brain and the body. Based on this chemical feedback loop, we think the way we feel and we feel the way we think. Therefore, we decide in that present moment who we are based on our thinking and feeling and determine if we are angry or suffering or inspired or negative and so on. After years of thinking those same thoughts and feelings, we create a memorized state of mind and declare an "I am" statement. I am angry, I am suffering, I am inspired, and so on. We are now defining ourselves as this state of mind and at this point, our thoughts and feelings have merged. We begin not only declaring our state of mind, but we start to say things like "I am a lazy person", or "I am a nervous person". We have created our personality state based on our thinking and feeling, based on outside experiences.

Breaking a Habit

When we think about a highly charged past emotional experience, the brain fires in the exact sequence and pattern as before; we are firing and wiring our brains to the past by reinforcing the circuits into more hardwired networks. When the body can remember better than the conscious mind, the body becomes the mind--this is called a habit. We could also say that the body becomes the subconscious mind, which as you'll remember, is a powerful 95% or our mind. With this in mind, we can begin to see why it's so hard to change. We may want to be happy, healthy, financially independent, and have wonderful relationships, but the experience of many years of suffering and the repeated cycle of those chemicals being processed, have subconsciously conditioned the body to be in a habitual state of pain and suffering or at the very least, in a stuck state. We are living in habit because we are no longer aware of what we are thinking, doing or feelings--we are unconscious. We must break this habit of being who we have become.

This is exactly what happened to me when in my ordinary world, I was ignoring my mind and body and heaping piles of stress onto my system for years until my body just gave out. What followed, were years of chronic pain that changed my brain. I was living every day in the habit of chronic pain and creating neural networks that when I moved a certain way or did anything strenuous, I would feel pain. Long after I healed my emotional and physical scars, my brain still needed to unwire those chronic pain signals. I still have to work daily on reprogramming my old chronic pain brain into a healthy thinking and feeling brain.

Neural Networks

I've mentioned neural networks being created in the brain. Before I became a life coach, I was an engineer in the telecommunications industry. I like to say that I single-handedly built the AOL network, which was basically a precursor to the internet. So, like Al Gore, I like to say that "I built the internet". All kidding aside, way back when I was engineering communication networks, we would install telephone switches (big computers) all over the world and would connect them with long distance telephone lines.

SIMPLE WELL DESIGNED TELEPHONE NETWORK. WHEN A SWITCH GOES DOWN, CALLS ARE TEMPORARILY RE-ROUTED.

Our networks were designed in a way that if one switch when down, the calls would automatically be re-routed to other working switches to complete the calls. Usually, the downed switch would reboot and come back up quickly or we would send someone to fix it. Once the switch came back up, any new calls would be routed over the normal route using that repaired switch. This worked great and kept any one switch or network route from being overloaded. Just like a normal functioning brain. But what would happen if, for some reason, that switch never came back up or got repaired? The calls would all be routed over that temporary backup route. The theory was that if a switch went down temporarily, the network would re-route traffic for a short time without any detrimental effects or dropped calls. But if all the traffic were to be re-routed over the backup route for a long time, it would not function properly because the network wasn't engineered that way. It would in affect become a hard-wired path for calls but wouldn't be as efficient or helpful to the network. Pretty soon the network just automatically route calls over this inefficient circuit.

Eventually though, what would happen is that we would just add more switches to the backup route and create a larger and more robust network based on this new route because it was sometimes easier to add a switch to the backup route then to fix the broken switch that caused the re-route in the first place. So, now our network looked different and there were very large phone circuits in an area that didn't need them there.

**DISTORTED NETWORK WITH AN ABNORMALLY
LARGE, BUT INEFFICIENT, CIRCUIT**

J. SCOTT MACMILLAN

So, now we have this distorted looking network with very large circuits or bandwidth in certain areas that didn't make sense. They worked great and tons of calls flowed over them, but it was costing us more money because it wasn't the most efficient use of our resources. Basically, we let the outside environment dictate how our network worked. We knew the most efficient way to create a network and that's how it started, but after letting some switches to stay offline and re-routed traffic, it created lopsided networks with huge circuits that could carry a lot of calls, but not in an efficient way.

What I have just described is what happens in our brains when we let the outside world dictate how we think, feel and act. Dr. Dispenza likes to refer to the phrase 'nerve cells that fire together, wire together'. The official name for this event is called Hebb's Law. It states that if you repeatedly activate the same nerve cells, then each time they turn on, it will be easier for them to fire in unison again and eventually, those neurons will develop a long-term relationship. So, just like my communication networks, when I say thoughts, behaviors or feelings are hardwired, I mean that clusters of neurons have fired together many times in the very same way and have organized themselves into specific patterns and connections. The more these networks of neurons fire, the more they wire into static routes of activity. Eventually, whatever the thoughts, behaviors or feelings included in those neural networks are, they will become an automatic unconscious habit. Just like the backup circuits of a communication network can re-route calls, our brains can re-route neurons to create neural networks based on either the way it was designed to efficiently run, or based on the outside world. What I am saying is that of course, you don't want to create neural networks based on the unpredictable and often negative outside world with all its potential problems, but rather, you want to create your own positive highly efficient and smooth running neural networks.

The good news is that since we created these crazy misguided and negative neural network loops, we can un-create them and put an end to letting the outside environment control our minds and lives. To do so though, we must fundamentally change the way we think, act and feel. Because the way we think, feel and act is called our personality and it's what creates our personal reality. Am I saying that to become our own heroes and live a purpose-driven life we must create a new personality? Absolutely! That's exactly what I'm saying. The good news is there are practical ways and steps to do it and I'll be here to guide you through it all.

The Dreamers

Think of any number of great historical figures like Abraham Lincoln, Martin Luther King, Nelson Mandela or even Michael Jackson and Michael Jordan. Do you know what they all had in common aside from greatness? They all had a dream or vision that was deep within them and was so present in their existence that they lived and breathed their destiny. They vividly saw in their minds what they would become or achieve or create ahead of it ever having happened. In other words, they behaved as if what they saw for their life was already a reality. They had no doubt that their vision would be real during their lives. When our thoughts and feelings are coherent, when our minds and our bodies work together, when our words, deeds, and actions are aligned, there is nothing that can't happen. Quantum physics demands it.

Change Your Thoughts, Change Your Life

Neuroscience has proven that we can change our brains – and therefore our behaviors, attitudes, and beliefs –just by thinking differently (in other words, without changing anything in our environment). Through mental rehearsal (repeatedly imagining performing an action), the circuits in the brain can reorganize themselves to reflect our objectives. We can make our thoughts so real that the brain changes to look like the event has already become a physical reality. Our thoughts can become our experience.

Athletes and sports psychologist have known this for years. Most high performing athletes visualize their performance in their minds prior to actually performing them on the court, field or course. They visualize every last detail of every swing, shot, catch or throw, done in perfect rhythm and form. As they do this their minds can't tell the difference between actually performing or mentally performing. If high performing athletes can do this, so can we to create our mission and purposeful life.

Most of us live in the past and resist living in a new future because our bodies are so habituated to memorizing the chemical records of our past experiences that they grow attached to these emotions. We become addicted to those familiar feelings. When we are in the midst of an experience, our brain receives information from the external environment through the senses (sight, smell, sound, taste, and touch). As that cumulative sensory data reaches the brain and is processed, networks of neurons arrange themselves into specific patterns, reflecting the external event, while the brain releases emotional chemicals. The more intense the experience, the more emotional chemicals will flood the body, and the more we will pay attention to whoever or whatever was in our external environment that caused the change. That event is now called a memory, and it includes the feelings and emotional chemical signatures of that event. Feelings and emotions are a chemical record of past experiences.

The only way we can change ourselves is to think beyond our past and how we feel. Accomplishing this feat is the great challenge of personal change. Thoughts and emotions are not bad, they are just the end products of experience. But if we are always reliving the past, we can't embrace new experiences.

Changing Our Genetics

Before we dive into the specifics of how we go about creating lasting change, let me talk about one more amazing area that was once believed to be static, like our brains. I'm talking about our physical health and our genes. Most people think we must live with the genes we were dealt with. This may be true of the DNA strands that we inherit, but the science of Epigenetics shows us that genes can change, or the gene function can change without a change in the DNA. We now know that the environment, by activating or deactivating particular genes, has the most effect on our health. According to Dr. Dispenza, less than 5% of all diseases today stem from single gene disorders. Whereas 95% of all illnesses are related to lifestyle choices, chronic stress, and toxic factors in the environment. This is amazing news because it shows that we have much more control over our health than was once believed. By changing our internal state of mind, we overcome the effects of a stressful or toxic environment, so that certain genes do not become activated. We may not be able to control all the conditions in our external environment, but we certainly have a choice in controlling our inner environment.

We now know that genes are as changeable as our brains. Just by changing our thoughts, feelings and emotions and making healthier lifestyle choices regarding nutrition and stress, we send our cells new signals, which can express new functions without changing the genetic code. Just like we can change who we have been, we can signal our genes to create beneficial health.

Living in Survival Mode - The Stress Response

By now, we've all heard of the stress response and how we were created with the ability to turn on what's called the fight or flight response. Every time we create an environment where the body is out of chemical balance, we create the stress response, which is how the body responds when it's in stress and what it does to return to equilibrium. We are the only animal that can turn on the fight or flight response by thought alone, even if that thought has nothing to do with our present reality or not. We can turn on that stress response in anticipation of the future. But even more devastating is the fact that we can produce the same stress response by thinking about an unhappy memory. Our bodies are either existing in the future or the past. No organism was designed to deal with the negative effects of stress when it is constantly turned on. When we can't turn off the stress response, we are headed for a breakdown in the body. Been there, done that, and it's not fun.

The overproduction of stress hormones creates emotions of anger, fear, envy and hatred, which can incite the feelings of aggression, frustration, anxiety, and insecurity and cause us to experience pain, suffering, sadness, hopelessness, and depression. The stress response forces us to focus on and obsess about the body, the environment and time. Thus, we begin to define our "self" within the confines of the physical realm; we become less spiritual, less conscious, less aware and less mindful. Living in survival mode causes us to focus on the .00001 percent instead of the 99.99999 percent of reality.

The other alternative is to live in creation. When we are in the midst of creating, we forget about ourselves. We dissociate from our known world and are no longer someone who associates our identity with certain things we own, or people we know, or certain tasks we do or places we have visited. We become self-less. We have moved beyond time and space and become pure awareness. Once we are no longer connected to our bodies and no longer focused on people, places or things in the external environment, we can enter the quantum field.

We have the ability to observe our own thoughts and self. We can decide that we no longer want to be, act, think or feel like we have been. This ability to self-reflect allows us to modify our behaviors so we can achieve something newer, better and greater.

Remember, energy flows where attention goes. To use our attention to empower our new life we must first figure out what we have already created in the old us. We need to look at our limiting beliefs about life, ourselves and others. Our lives are dictated by our beliefs. Our beliefs are the thoughts we keep consciously or unconsciously, accepting them as the law in our lives. Whether we are aware of them or not, they still affect our reality. We must go in deep and look at things we probably have been unaware of before. We must unearth our subconscious thoughts, reflexive behaviors and automatic emotional reactions, and put them under a microscope and determine if they are true or not. Most likely, a lot of our limiting beliefs were created when we were very young, 0-6 years of age, and they are most likely not true.

The purpose of becoming self-aware is so that we will no longer allow any thoughts, actions or emotions we don't want to experience to pass by our awareness. We want to consciously inhibit any of these limiting beliefs so we don't continue firing and wiring the old neural networks. We can begin to prune away the old neural hardware. The goal here is to unlearn the old personality so we can free up space for the new personality and new future that we will be creating.

One of the ways we are going to create our new personality is to set aside time to think about a new way of thinking and feeling. We can imagine fresh new possibilities by asking ourselves important questions about what we want and who we want to be and what we want to change in our lives. Once we have figured out what we want to be, we can begin to mentally rehearse these new ways of thinking and feeling. By continually practicing these thinking and feeling sessions, we will start rewiring ourselves neurologically to a new mind. The more we can "re-mind" ourselves, the more we'll change our brains and our lives.

Meditate to Change

Let's look at how we can circumvent our natural tendencies to create thoughts and feelings from external experiences. This process is backed by real science and is not a 'fake it until you make it' trick. We can create a new reality by creating a new way of thinking and being. If you have ever thought of something that hasn't happened yet, like what you're going to have for dinner this evening, to the speech you need to give tomorrow at work, you can create your new reality. Your thinking about those future events was to the exclusion of everything else that was happening to you at that very moment. Your body started to move into that being just by your thinking it alone. You probably started to feel hungry after thinking about your dinner, or your body may have tensed up as you thought about the speech you had to give. Your mind and body started to be one. Can you use this same concept to create the reality you want and become your own hero? You absolutely can, and you can do it via the meditation process I am going to show you. Meditation allows us to change our brains, bodies and our state of mind. We can make these changes from the comfort of our couch or chair with no external experience whatsoever. Through meditation, we can install new neurological hardwired neural networks.

The meditative process allows you to create a new state of mind and being by bringing together all the information learned and wired synaptically into your brain about what it means to be the kind of person you want to become. For example, if you wanted the new you to be a happy and content person, all you must do is think about being happy and content, satisfied and at peace. After all, you know what happiness looks and feels like; you've had past experiences with it yourself. Now you get to pick and choose from the knowledge and experience to create the new ideal of yourself.

Once you have created those thoughts and feelings in your mind, you have activated new circuits in new ways to create a holographic image that gives you a model to follow in creating your future reality. You simply must use your knowledge and experience of the feeling or emotion you want to create, to create an emotional state in your meditation.

How will you know that your meditations are working? Because you will feel different from living and committing to the process. You will feel differently and act differently, and signs from the Universe/God/Creator will reign down on you in unexpected ways. If you feel the same as you did before, then nothing has happened in the Universal field. Your same thoughts and feeling are reproducing the same electromagnetic signal to the field. You must stay committed and not get up from your meditation session until you are that new person with new thoughts, feelings and emotions that you have selected in advance. You are now the designer of your life. Your job is to live into your new reality by continually doing your meditations You're changing the inside of you, which will eventually change the outside of you. You have broken that old Newtonian concept of something external controlling your thoughts, actions and emotions.

If you have tried to live by the law of attraction before but never achieved the life you wanted, it's possible that you've been living by a negative memorized emotion that has become so much a part of your identity on a subconscious level that you cannot feel any other way. Doing the exercises and meditations that I am about to show you will finally break you free of these limiting and life crippling beliefs once and for all.

CHAPTER 8
FOLLOW YOUR BLISS - THE TRANSFORMATIONAL LADDER

Joseph Campbell tells us that the true hero find's their bliss and gives their gifts to the world. That's the ultimate treasure claimed from the courageous Hero's Journey. Now that we understand that we can be the hero of our lives, how a healthy human psychologically progresses in life, and how it's possible to create this new hero, let's find your bliss and complete your Hero's Journey. The following exercises will help peel back the layers of what I call the transformational ladder and create your new self with new more empowering thoughts and beliefs.

You can either fill in the answers here in this chapter or print out Appendix A: which has all the exercises in one place.

The Transformational Ladder

No matter if you are stuck in the middle of your Hero's Journey or have completed many Hero's Journey's there is always room for improvement. Human suffering comes from the illusion that we are not enough. This is universal for humans and it starts in young childhood when we are completely at the mercy of our parents to support us in life.

The transformational ladder will guide you from defining your limiting behaviors, down through the limiting stories you tell yourself, and what emotions are causing the main limiting beliefs that were created by original life triggering events. With this information, you will be ready to move onto climbing back up the ladder with new empowering beliefs, emotions, stories and behaviors, and become the hero of your life.

The exercises below will help you figure out where you are stuck in life and will give you insight on how to get unstuck and move forward in your journey. If you have completed the exercises in section one on the Hero's Journey, you can already see how your life has unfolded into your journey. Now it's time to go deep and define what you want to change in your life and why. It's your job to look back on your life and figure out where things may have gone wrong or where unfortunate circumstances took place, and what meaning you attached to those life events. As you use the exercises to uncover your personal growth pattern, you will begin to see yourself as the hero of your own life and how your life has shaped your journey so far. With this knowledge, you will peel back the onion of your transformational ladder and sit with this knowledge for a while. With a clear understanding of how your past life might have contributed to your limiting beliefs and actions, you will rebuild your ideal hero life by climbing back up the ladder with new and more empowering stories, feelings, thoughts and emotions.

Uncovering Where You Are Stuck

Where are you stuck in your life? These are areas where you are most frustrated, annoyed, disappointed, feeling helpless. The primary feelings of being stuck are powerlessness, hiding, and frustration.

Remember the first step to change is admitting you are stuck.

Some examples are:

- Stuck in a relationship you know isn't working.
- Stuck in a job that is sucking the life out of you.
- Maybe you have lost your connection to your faith.

- You never have enough money
- You are overweight
- You are out of shape
- Your family doesn't support you
- You have chronic pain

List Where You Are Stuck:

1.
2.
3.
4.
5.

Now take a few minutes to reflect on these stuck areas of your life above by answering the following questions.

- **How have you ignored these stuck areas or used them as excuses?**
  -
  -
  -

- **How long have these stuck areas been with you? Are you repeating a pattern?**
  -
  -
  -

- **Can you remember the first time when you felt stuck in these areas?**
  -
  -
  -

- **Do you believe that staying stuck in these areas benefited you in any way?**
  -
  -
  -

- **Do you have any relationships in your life that support you being stuck in these areas?**
  -
  -
  -

Why Must You Change?

Now let's get clear on why you must change. What have you missed out on because you let fear and apathy rule your life?

List them here. I have missed:

- **Romance:**
  -

- **Career:**
  -

- **Health:**
  -

- **Spirituality:**
  -

- **Relationships:**
  -

- **Finances:**
  -

- **Contribution:**
  -

- **Add Your Own Category:**

Make a list of all the things you want in your life. What do you want to feel? What do you want to do with your life? What things do you want to have in your life? Who do you want to love?

1.
2.
3.
4.
5.

Write out why you must commit to changing now (Be as detailed as possible.)

_____

_____

_____

_____

Now answer these questions:

- What is the worst that could happen if I don't change now?
  -
  -

- What's the worst thing that could happen if I decide to change now?
  -
  -

- **Has the Universe/God/Creator tried to get my attention recently? What were the signs?**
  -
  -

Now that you have identified where you are stuck, why you must change and what you want out of life, you will dive into your emotions, and what limiting beliefs, stories and events have held you back.

The difference between a belief, an emotion, a story and a behavior is when you have an early trauma or crisis in your life, a belief is the meaning that you created from that traumatic event. Beliefs create emotions or a felt sense in the body. Your emotions create your stories or how you describe your circumstances. Your stories create your behaviors or how you repeatedly react to your circumstances.

We are wired to assign meaning to what happens to us in life. The amazing thing, though, is that no one else can assign meaning to our life events, only we can do that. That should make you feel very very hopeful.

Your Limiting Stories, Thinking and Beliefs

What Are The Stories You Tell Yourself?

Our behaviors are usually driven by the stories we tell ourself. We don't just do things randomly. Our thoughts create our behavior. Every behavior was first a thought or story.

There are all kinds of stories that hold you back. Common ones are:

- The world is not a safe place
- I'm too old
- I'm too fat
- I don't have enough time

- I don't have enough money
- I'm too young
- I'm not safe
- Life will never get better
- This is all I'm worth
- I've always been this way
- I don't feel I can be my true self
- My children's happiness is more important than my own
- My parents don't approve of who I am
- Life doesn't support me
- I'm cursed
- This works for other people but not me.

You may see your stories above or have different ones. What stories are you telling yourself?

Write them down.

1.
2.
3.
4.
5.

Where did your limiting stories came from? As you do this, remember not to beat yourself up. Be kind and and gentle with yourself as you look at the hard parts of your life, and trust the process. Go back and read what you wrote about the stories you tell yourself. Allow yourself to soak them in.

Don't push them away.

Then ask yourself, where was the first time I remember hearing this story?

Some examples are:

- My parents
- Significant others
- Religion
- Bosses
- Brothers or sisters
- The media
- Bullies in school
- Your friends
- Extended family members
- People you look up to
- Role models
- Negative voices in my head

Then try and think about the actual words that these people said to you.

Some examples are:

- Finish your plate, there are starving kids in India
- You'll never amount to anything
- You're be just like your mother/father
- Children should be seen and not heard
- No one in this family has ever gone to college, what makes you think you can?
- Don't every air your dirty laundry in public

List your top 5 times when you first heard these limiting stories and what they were.

1.
2.
3.
4.
5.

Identify Limiting Beliefs

Beliefs are more powerful than stories because beliefs are in many ways the origin of the stories we tell about life, because beliefs are based on the meaning we gave past events in our life. In other words, belief determines how we see or perceive and event. Like a filter. And a story is the account of what happened or what will happen based on your beliefs.

Some Examples Are:

- I'll never get a new job
- No one ever listens to me
- He always makes me feel angry
- Everyone uses me
- I want to call it quits
- Today is a bad day for me, so why bother trying to change it.
- It's her fault that my life is this way
- I'm really not that smart
- I honestly can't change. Maybe it would be better to start another time
- I don't feel like it
- My life sucks
- I hate my situation with _____
- I'll never make a difference. I can't
- _____ does not like me
- I have to work harder than most people.
- It's my genetics. I am just like my mother

Review the stories you tell yourself and where they came from and turn them into belief statements.

List your limiting beliefs here:

1.
2.

3.

4.

5.

Uncovering Your Triggering Life Events

We are going to go back to a time of hurt, a time you have pushed away for so long, a time that you may even have pretended didn't happen and that you don't want to talk about. It is your moment or moments of trauma, pain and original hurt.

These triggering life events are moments in our past when something happened and we decided to form a belief about the world. They come from all kinds of places. They can be something as simple as being left behind at school, a kid calling you fat, or the tone in which a parent said something to you as a child. Or your they could be more extreme, like sexual, emotional, or physical abuse.

The majority of these triggering life events start before the age of 10. Because they are never addressed or worked through, these limiting beliefs carry themselves into adulthood. In order to change your story these triggering life events must be seen with new eyes. It's time to uncover how these limiting beliefs were created to protect yourself long ago and step into your more powerful life. It may take running through this process a few times to find all the triggering life events.

Here is a list of common triggering life events.

- Sexual abuse
- Physical abuse
- Emotional abuse
- Violent family members
- Being required to be perfect, rather than yourself
- Being abandoned by on for both parents
- A parents addiction
- Needed to be the caregiver of your parent as a child

- Other people condemning you
- Being made fun of at school
- Witnessing violence
- The death of a loved one
- Not being recognized by your father
- Not being nurtured by your mother

Go back and read your top five limiting beliefs. Take a minute to let the emotions to wash over you.

Then ask yourself "What triggering life events happened in my life that made me believe these things?"

1.
2.
3.
4.
5.

Your Negative Emotions

Go back to the list you created of the limiting thinking, stories and beliefs that hold you back. Reread them. Then bring your awareness to your body. How are you feeling as you read these stories, thoughts and beliefs? And where are you feeling it? Some people feel these deep strong emotions in there stomach, jaw or weakness in the legs. Pay attention to where you feel them.

Right now we are just going to sit with those feelings rather than acting on them. If this brings up panic, fear and shame, that is okay. There is nothing wrong with you. Remember you are not your feelings and emotions.

I usually feel my deep emotions in my throat and solar plexus. Where do you feel your deep emotions?

Think of all the times your limiting stories, thoughts and beliefs that have held you back. Look at the pain you've caused others. Look at the pain you've caused yourself. Look how you have kept yourself small, how you've put others first, denied your own worth and intuition. Look back over your hero's journey life and see how you've held yourself back. Notice how this makes you feel and where you feel it in your body.

Naming Your Emotions

Now that you have gotten in touch with your emotions list five emotions that you feel as a result of these limiting behaviors and stories and the areas in your body where you feel them.

If it's hard to access your emotions, or if you're getting frustrated that you aren't feeling anything, this is good. You're feeling frustrated. Where do you feel that in your body? Just because you don't feel the emotions you think you should be feeling doesn't mean you can't feel. Your job is to go with whatever is present in the here and now.

Some common emotions are:

- Anger
- Hate, Powerlessness
- Guilt
- Shame
- Sadness
- Unworthiness
- Betrayal
- Regret
- Depression
- Stress
- Self-doubt
- Lack of belonging
- Resentment

List your emotions here:

1. I feel _____ in my _____
2. I feel _____ in my _____
3. I feel _____ in my _____
4. I feel _____ in my _____
5. I feel _____ in my _____

These are difficult things to feel, and you may want to turn back. But don't. Stay with it. These feelings will pass and fade away. These emotions do not control you. In fact, feeling them is the first step toward setting yourself free

Identify Limiting Thinking

Next ask yourself - How do I think when I feel this way? For example if you want to get rid of the feeling of shame. Ask yourself "What is my attitude when I feel shame?" You might say you are scared or timid or quiet and shy. An attitude is a series of thoughts connected to a feeling. You need to define the habit that has been created by this emotion.

Some Examples Are:

- Competitive
- Blaming
- Desperate
- Lacking
- Overly intellectual
- Lazy
- Dishonest
- Controlling
- Needy
- Sensitive
- Insensitive

List your top 5.

1.
2.
3.
4.
5.

Most of your actions, behaviors and choices have been equal to these feelings and has made you act in predictable ways. Just be with these emotional attitudes without doing anything. Just observe them.

Limiting Behaviors That Hold You Back

The difference between a belief, an emotion, a story and a behavior is when you have an early trauma or crisis in your life, a belief is the meaning that you created from that traumatic event. Beliefs create emotions or a felt sense in the body. Your emotions create your stories or how you describe your circumstances. Your stories create your behaviors or how you repeatedly react to your circumstances.

We are wired to assign meaning to what happens to us in life. The amazing thing, though, is that no one else can assign meaning to our life events, only we can do that. That should make you feel very very hopeful.

List the 5 behaviors that hold you back. These are the behaviors you blame yourself for doing and yet you can't seem to find a way past them.

Some of these behaviors might be:

- Self-sabotage
- Over-eating
- Blaming Others
- Withdrawing or hiding
- Lying

- Abusing porn
- Abusing gambling
- Cheating on your partner

List your limiting behaviors here:

1.
2.
3.
4.
5.

Admitting Who You Are

Acknowledge your true self rather than the self you show to other people. Allow yourself to be vulnerable. Tell the Universe/God/Creator who you have been and what you want to change about yourself, and admit what you are hiding.

Owning up to who we really are and what our past mistakes have been and asking to be accepted are among the most challenging things for us to do as humans. This works because we are admitting our faults and failures to our higher power and not to another similarly flawed human.

Close your eyes and become still and begin to tell this higher power who you have been. Share the details of the stories that you have carried around with you.

Some Examples Are:

- I am afraid of falling in love because it hurts too much
- I pretend I am happy, but I am really suffering because I am lonely
- I do not want anyone to know that If feel so guilty, so I lie about myself

- I lie to people so that they like me and so I won't feel so unloved and unworthy.
- I can't stop feeling self-pity. I think, act, and feel this way all day long because I do not know how else I can feel.
- I have felt like a failure most of my life, so I try extra to be a success

Write down what comes up.

_____

_____

_____

_____

Creating The New You - Climbing Back Up The Transformational Ladder

Up till now you've worked at identifying your limited thinking and pruning away old synaptic connections. Now it's time to sprout new ones so that the new mind you create will become the platform of who you will be in your future. Let's find your bliss and create a new you. Your daily meditations, contemplations, and rehearsals will be like tending to a garden to yield a great expression of the new you. You should fall in love with the vision of who you are becoming. Love is a higher frequency emotion than those in survival emotions that allowed the negative and limiting beliefs to control your unconscious thinking.

Below are a series of open ended questions that will cause you to think in different ways than you normally think and to entertain new possibilities, - This turns on your frontal lobe. You are creating the platform of the new self by forcing the brain to fire in novel ways.

Write down answers to as many questions seems relevant to you. After you complete the answers, review, reflect, analyze and think about all the possibilities your answers raise. You will then be climbing the transformational ladder with new beliefs, emotions, stories and behaviors.

How Do I Want To Think

- What is the greatest ideal of myself?
  -
  -

- Who in history do I admire?
  -
  -

- Whom do I want to model?
  -
  -

- How would I be if I were like them?
  -
  -

- What would I say to myself if I were this new person I want to be?
  -
  -

- How would I talk to others if I were changed.
  -
  -

How Do I Want To Act?

- How would this new person act?
  -
  -

- What would I do?
  -
  -

- How do I see myself behaving?
  -
  -

- How would I speak as this new expression of self?
  -
  -

- What is my new attitude?
  -
  -

- What do I want to believe about me?
  -
  -

- How do I want to be perceived?
  -
  -

- What would I say to myself if I was this person?
  -
  -

- How would this person act?
  -
  -

- What would he or she do?
  -
  -

- How do I see myself behaving?
  -
  -

- How would I speak as this new person?
  -
  -

How Do I Want To Feel?

- How would this new self be?
  -
  -

- What would I feel?
  -
  -

- What would my energy be like as this new ideal?
  -
  -

Now that you have brainstormed how you want to think, feel and act differently, it's time to get specific on your new empowering stories, beliefs, thinking and behaviors.

Review you limiting stories, beliefs, thinking and behaviors and rewrite them into positives statements.

New Empowering Stories That Move Your Forward

List your top 5.

1.
2.
3.
4.
5.

New Empowering Beliefs That Move Your Forward

List your top 5:

1.
2.
3.
4.
5.

New Empowering Thinking That Move Your Forward

List your top 5:

1.
2.
3.
4.
5.

New Empowering Behaviors That Move Your Forward

List your top 5:

1.
2.
3.
4.
5.

Hero Life Exercise:

Step 1: What is Your Hero Moment?

Imagine a time in your life when you accomplished or did something that made you feel absolutely incredible. A time where you felt empowered, confident, happy, and full of energy. A time in your life that you felt like you can do anything you put your mind to.

It can be ANY time in your life. When you were a kid, hitting a home run, acing a test, leaving your job, getting a big check, accomplishing something significant, falling in love, speaking on stage, or doing something you've never done before and crushing it.

_____

_____

_____

_____

Step 2: Refine it, what was the most powerful part of your hero life moment?

Refine it all the way down to one specific moment. Examples: receiving an award, the feeling of crossing home plate after the game winning home run, the sound of the crowd during a standing ovation, the feeling of looking at an "A" on your final exam.

_____

_____

_____

_____

Step 3: Attach a meaning to it, why is that moment so significant for you?

What does it mean to you? Examples, you accomplished something great before and you can do it again. You stepped outside your comfort zone and you can do it again. You can do anything you put your mind to.

_____

_____

_____

_____

Step 4: Physiologically how did you feel during your Hero moment?

What did you feel, how did you stand, how were you breathing, what did you hear?

_____

_____

_____

_____

If you can have that happen to you back then, what is holding you back now? What if you could achieve something this amazing now?

What if you thought about this moment every day and recreated that physiological response in your body? You can leverage this for any project, event or anytime you want to get pumped up empowered to take action.

Discovering Purpose and Passion

Passion and purpose are similar but distinct. They are connected and seductive to us all.

The following exercises will help draw out the purpose and passion that resides within you. Don't come at this with preconceived ideas of what your purpose is or should be or what others think it should be.

Take your time with these questions. The answers you seek will be revealed when you go inward with calmness, patience and vulnerability.

Think about what makes you tear up?

- When you are emotionally moved, it is a sign of what resonates within you, either good or bad, happy or sad. We all have something that triggers our emotions and feelings. Describe what that is for you.

_____

_____

_____

_____

What makes you angry and annoyed?

- What kinds of things make you really mad and sometimes pushes you over the top?
- When you declare what makes you angry you are leaving clues as to what you are passionate about.

_____

_____

_____

_____

What charges and recharges you?

- What inspires and motivates you?
- Is it nature? Is it when you are being creative? Do you like working in groups or by yourself? Does music inspire you? What kind?
- The answers to this question are closely connected to your purpose and passion.

_____

_____

_____

_____

What are you better at than anyone else you know?

- This is when you are in your flow zone and quite often lose track of them when you're doing this.

_____

_____

_____

_____

What can people count on you to always do?

- In your family, what is it that you always do?
- At work, what are you the go to person for?
- This is where you walk your talk and find it easy to do.
- People have been telling you this your whole life.

_____

_____

_____

_____

When will you be worthy?

- What needs to happen for you to feel truly worthwhile?
  Remember we are hardest on ourselves.
- How will you know when you have "arrived?" When will your
  credibility be irrefutable?

_____

_____

_____

_____

What gift will you share with the world?

- Think about where your pain and suffering lives.
- Think about the areas that you want to hide .
- It may also be connected to your deepest desires.

_____

_____

_____

_____

Who or what would you die for?

- What means the most you? Who would you make the ultimate sacrifice for?
- When you know what you would die for it grants you the wisdom of knowing what to live for.
- Think about what's in it for you?

_____

_____

_____

_____

When your time is up what would your final wish be?

- You're not allowed to ask for more time.
- How will you use it?
- What will it be for?
- Who will benefit?
- When all you have is one wish left, your answer will be very revealing. Your purpose and passion are rooted in your values.

_____

_____

_____

_____

How do you want to be remembered?

- When you think about this, what would honor your memory the most?
- What stories would you most like to hear told about you at your funeral?
- The answers to this question are what are most important to you. These are the traits and attributes you value the most in life.
- This is how you want to live your life

_____

_____

_____

_____

Your passion and purpose are in these answers. You are the hero of your own life.

Rehearsing The New You

You've unpacked your limiting thinking, figured out why and created new empowering thinking as you climbed back up the transformational ladder. You have figured out your mission and what you're passionate about. Now it's time to take these new empowering views, follow your bliss and create the hero of your life. This part of the exercise will include creating powerful daily personal meditations and contemplations.

- Hold the image of you being or doing the things that you want this new you to do. You are the quantum observer, commanding matter to conform to your intentions.
- With clarity, hold the image of each manifestation in your mind for a few seconds, and then let it go into the quantum to be executed by a great mind.

- Give up trying to figure out how or when or where or with whom, leave those details to a mind that knows so much more than you do. And know that your creation will come in a way that you will least expect so that will surprise you and leave no doubt that this came from a higher order.

When you are unconsciously skilled at something, that means you just do it without having to place a great deal of conscious thought or attention to the activity. This is what you want to have happen. You want to practice being the new you so much that it becomes unconscious. The keys for you to focus on are Frequency, Intensity, and Duration. The more you do it, the easier it gets. The better you can focus and concentrate, the easier it will be for you to tap into that particular mind the next time. The longer you can linger in the thoughts, and emotions of your new ideal, without letting your mind wander to extraneous stimulus the more you will memorize new thoughts and feelings.

Creating A New Reality

Your new personality should create a new reality. When you are being someone else, you naturally will have a different life. The new identity is no longer emotionally anchored to known situations in your life that keep recycling the same circumstances; therefore it is a perfect place from which to envision a new destiny. This is the place you want to be to create your hero life.

The reason your past intensions hardly every manifested is that you were trying to hold a mindful intention while being lost in lower emotions such as guilt, shame, sadness, unworthiness, anger or fear connect to the old self. It was those feelings that were governing your thoughts and attitude. The 5% of your conscious mind was fighting against the 95% subconscious. Thinking one way and feeling another cannot produce results.

Creating a New Destiny

Now that you have released that old energy from the body, what do you want? Do you want to heal an area of you body or life? Do you want a loving relationship, a more satisfying career, a new car? Is your dream to write a book, to send your kids to college or yourself go back to school? From a new state of mind, body and gratitude; in a greater more coherent energy, see these images in your mind of what you want to create in your new life. Craft the specific future events you want to experience, by observing them into physical reality. You as the quantum observer are commanding matter to conform to your intentions. With clarity you will hold the image of each manifestation in your mind for a few seconds, and the let it go into the quantum field to be executed by your Universe/God?Creator.

Finally, give up trying to figure out how or when or where or with whom. Leave those details to a mind that nows so much more than you do. And know that your creation will come in a way that you will least expect, that will surprise you and leave no doubt that it came from a higher mind.

Write down what you want now that you are the new you.

- _____
- _____
- _____
- _____

It might be helpful to create 6 month goals from this list. By putting dates on when you expect to have or be these new ideas you are giving the quantum field even more information to help it manifest with you. Of course you still need to be surprised as to how or even when these events will occur. In fact these areas might be manifested way before your goal date.

Again, be as specific as you can be in what you want so you can visualize it and feel the joy and emotion of having achieved it in your life.

You are now ready to start your meditations. Now that you have worked through the transformational ladder, created a new you and made your six months goals, it's now time to put it all together into one mediation that you can do every day.

Meditation Recap

Part I The Induction Phase:

This is where you relax the body and mind enough to move into an Alpha or Theta wave. The best way to do this is to do a guided body relaxation meditation. Progressive muscle relaxing is a great way to get the mind into Alpha or Theta waves which are extremely conducive to the power of suggestion. This is essentially what hypnosis therapist do.

Part II Reminding Yourself who you Don't Want to Be:

Pick one emotion (at a time) and associated thoughts, feelings, actions and behaviors that you want to be rid of. Remind yourself of the emotions, feelings and behaviors you use to think and feel and ask the creator to take this emotion away from you. You can find this list in your Transformational Ladder exercises.

Part III Redirecting:

Think of 3 times during the day you might lapse into thinking or being in that negative emotion and then you will say CHANGE! Out loud.

Part IV Creating The New You:

Take what you have answered in the creating the new you exercises and feel into the new you. How you will think, do and act. Think about being like this new person. Picture yourself acting and doing and saying what this new you would say and do.

Part V Visualizing What The New You Wants:

Picture the images in your mind and feel how you would feel with the new areas in your life. What's going on around you, what are people saying or doing with you. Feel the emotion of having and doing this new behavior.

Part VI Release The Vision:

Release your new vision of you to Universe/God/Creator and ask for a a sign that you made a connection with the Devine.

Part VII Give Thanks:

Give thanks for having or being this new person. Be in so much gratitude and live in that gratitude all day long.

Part VIII Live As If:

Live the rest of the day as if you are that new person and in such gratitude for the life you are living as this new person with this new item or behavior.

SECTION THREE
QUANTUM MEDITATIONS

CHAPTER 9
QUANTUM REPROGRAMMING MEDITATION

Guided Alpha/Theta Meditation - Induction

There are various ways to get into an Alpha/Theta state. A standard breathing meditation can do it for some, while others might need guided progressive muscle relaxation with music to get there.

Here is a simple guided progressive muscle relaxation meditation that you can use, or find any good guided meditation to get into an Alpha/Theta wave state.

This induction meditation is adapted from the work of Glen Harrold.

You can download this meditation set to peaceful background music at www.betheheroofyourlife.com/downloads

Induction

Take a minute to get settled and comfortable in your chair or sitting position. Take a few deep breaths to relax. Gently close your eyes and continue to take deep breaths. With your eyes closed, feel into your surroundings. Feel into your body and the places your body touches-- the chair or floor. Feel your feet flat on the floor. Feel your seat in the chair and where your back hits the chair. Feel your hands resting on your lap. Now, take a moment to hear any sounds in the room, both inside and out.

Let any cares or worries drift away now as this is your time to relax and be. Now, begin to focus on your breathing as you inhale and exhale. Be with each breath for its full duration. Notice the rise and fall of your chest and stomach with each breath. Now, as you breathe in, feel the air hit the back of your throat and your lungs filling with air. As you breathe out, feel your body soften, releasing any tension. Allow your body to feel more relaxed and more peaceful with each breath. Enjoy the simplicity of this moment. Use your breath to anchor yourself to the present moment. Now, bring your attention to your face and feel any tension, and let it dissolve. Be aware of your head and notice the tiny muscles around your eyes and feel any tension drift away. Now, focus on your jaw, allowing it to relax with your teeth apart, releasing any tension.

Now, move your awareness to your shoulders and into your upper arms, your elbows, forearms and wrists. Sense the back of your hands, your palm, and your fingers.

Now, draw your attention to the back of the shoulders, following the arch from your upper back down to your lower back and to your hips. Allow the earth below your feet to draw you down into a grounded sensation. You feel grounded and centered.

Move your focus now to your thighs and down to your knees, your calf muscles, your shins ankles and feet, and down to your heels and to your toes and all the way to the tips of your toes. Just relax. You feel centered and balanced.

Now, focus your awareness on your body as a whole, and rest for a moment. You're feeling very safe and secure now. Now, sense the energy field around your entire body. You may even sense its vibration and color. As you focus on your whole body and your energy field, acknowledge any feelings or sensations as they come into your being. Imagine any tension, fear or stress dissolving away. Just letting go.

Now, I want you to imagine sitting near a gentle stream on a beautiful warm summer's day. There is lush green grass all around you, and you feel a pleasant and refreshing breeze against your skin as you enjoy these beautiful surroundings. If you ever had any fears of water, they fade away now. This is a magical healing place, a place where you feel safe and secure and at peace. Listen to the sound of the trickling stream as the sun sparkles on the surface of the water. The sound of trickling water fascinates you. It brings your awareness to the present moment. It feels like time is standing still.

As you continue to gaze at the water, you watch the gentle ebb and flow of the stream. Notice a few leaves floating on the surface of the water. As you watch the leaves moving slowly down the stream, notice any thoughts that may enter your mind. sAs they enter, mentally place each thought on a single leaf. As they come into your awareness, place your thoughts onto the leaves, one at a time. Then, watch as they pass by and float along the stream and out of view. It doesn't matter if they are happy or sad thoughts or where they came from; simply acknowledge them and let them go. Simply relax and just be in the present moment. If a thought comes into your mind, simply place it on a leaf and watch it flow downstream and out of sight.

Long pause HERE.

Now, drift away in a state of blissful presence and the gentle sounds will continue to wash over you. You feel completely refreshed and relaxed and have a deep sense of peace and well-being.

Now that you are totally relaxed and in Alpha state, gently transition into the next part of the meditation.

Declaring the Emotions You Want to Change and Reminding Yourself Who You No Longer Want to Be

This meditation is adapted from the work of Dr. Joe Dispenza

Now, say the emotions you want to change out loud and free them from your body, as well as your environment. Say them now...

Make sure that no thought, behavior, or feeling can cause you to return to the old self. To make sure, remember how you used to think when you felt that way? What did you say to yourself? What voice did you listen to that you no longer want to accept as your reality? Observe those thoughts.. How did you once behave? How did you speak? Become conscious of these unconscious states to such an extent that they will never go unnoticed by you again.

Remind yourself who you no longer want to be, how you no longer want to think, how you no longer want to behave, and how you no longer want to feel. Become familiar with all aspects of the old personality, and just observe. With firm intention, make a choice to no longer be that person, and let the energy of your decisions become a memorable experience.

Redirecting

Now it's time to practice redirecting limited thoughts as they creep up during the day. Imagine scenarios in your life where you could start to feel like the old self again. Then say STOP! out loud.

Become aware of a person or situation where you could easily fall into an old behavioral pattern. Say STOP!

Now picture yourself in an event in your life where there is a possibility to fall short of your ideal. Say STOP!

Now, picture a situation where you are thinking and feeling in an unconscious way. Say STOP!

The rewards of being healthy and happy are so much more important than returning to the old self. Those emotions have never been loving to you. Every time you change your state, you know that old nerve cells are no longer firing together, and no longer wiring together, and that you're not turning on the same genes in the same ways.

Creating the New You

Now that you absolutely know what you want to change, let's create the new hero of your life.

What is the greatest expression of yourself that you can be? How would you, as this great person, think and act? How will you live? How will you love? What does greatness feel like? Move into a new state of being. It is time to change your energy and broadcast a whole new electromagnetic signature. When you change your energy, you change your life. Let your thoughts become the experience, and let that experience produce elevated emotions so that your body begins to emotionally believe that the future you, is already living now.

Allow yourself to turn on new genes in new ways, and signal the body emotionally ahead of the actual event. Allow yourself to fall in love with the new ideal; open your heart and begin to recondition your body to a new mind.

Let the inward experience become a mood, then a temperament, and finally a new personality. Move into a new state of being. You can't get up as the same person who sat down. You must feel gratitude so that your body begins to change ahead of the actual event, and accept that the new ideal already is you. Become it. To be empowered, to be free, to be unlimited, to be creative, to be a genius, to be divine--this is who you are.

Once you feel this way, memorize this feeling; remember this feeling. This is who you truly are.

Now let go and release it into the unlimited quantum field for a moment, and just let go.

You must wire that new mind again and recondition the body to a new emotion. What's the greatest expression of yourself? Allow yourself to begin to think like this ideal again.

What would you say to yourself, how would you walk, how would you breathe, how would you move, how would you live, what would you feel? Allow yourself to emotionally feel like this new self, so much that you begin to move into a new state of being.

Who do you want to be when you open your eyes? Feel empowered once again. This is where you create a new destiny. From this elevated state of mind and body, it is time to command matter as a quantum observer of your new reality. Feel invincible, powerful, inspired, grateful and overjoyed.

From this new state of being, form a picture of some event you want to experience and let the images become the reality of your future. Observe that reality and allow the particles as waves of probability collapse into an event called or experience in your life. See it, command it, hold it, and then move to the next image.

That future event must find you because you created it with your own energy. Let yourself go and create the future you want in certainty, trust and knowingness. Do not analyze or try to figure out how it is going to happen. It is not your job to control the outcome. It is your task to design your ideal self and leave the details to the Universe/God/Creator. As you see your future as the observer, simply bless your life with your own energy. From a state of gratitude, be one with your destiny from a new state of mind and body. Give thanks for a new life.

Feel how you will feel when these things manifest in your life because living in a state of gratitude is living in a state of receivership. Feel like your prayers are already answered. Finally, it's time to turn to that power within you and ask it for a sign in your life. If today you emulated this Universe/God/Creator mind, observed all of life into form, and made contact with it, then it has been observing your efforts and intentions and should show up in your life. Know that it is real, that it exists, and that you now have a two-way communication with it. Ask that this sign from the Universe/God/Creator come in a way that you would least expect and in a way that surprises you and leaves you with no doubt that this new experience has come from your Universe/God/Creator, so that you are inspired to do it again. Ask for a sign now.

Now, go and live the rest of your day as if you are that new person and be grateful for the life you are living as this new person.

Now, move your awareness back to a new body in a new environment and in a whole new line of time. And when you are ready, bring your awareness back up to Beta. Then you can open your eyes.

SECTION FOUR
APPENDICES

APPENDIX A
EXERCISES

Complete a timeline of your life up until now. List the most significant events. This isn't a detailed list of your whole life, but it will give you a good idea of where you were in the 12 stages of the hero's journey exercise below.

Example Timeline

Year	Life Event
1962	Born in Helena Montana
1980	Graduated from Flathead High school
1986	Graduated from University Of Montana with a psychology degree
1987	Packed up my Honda Civic and drove across the country to start my life in Washington D.C.
1987	Got my first real job at Tymnet - Living in Northern Virginia

Your Turn:

Year	Life Event

Your Hero's Journey Exercise

Read about the 12 stages of the hero's journey and what they represent. Then place your life events into each stage. Make sure to identify not only what was going on in your life at this time but what the significance of this time or your life meant to you.

Don't worry if you can't identify a part of your life that doesn't fit into a particular stage. You can skip it or come back to it later.

Decide as early in the process as you can, if you are going to list out your entire life until now into one big Hero's Journey or you think you may have had more than one already. Remember that you can have multiple events in your life that may be in one stage, for example you may have had many calls to adventure but refused the call many times before actually crossing the threshold. I find it helpful to try and fit your entire life so far into one hero's journey. You may, and usually will, find that you are in the middle of your hero's journey with a few stages yet to move through.

The following questions will help you determine what preparation stage you need help with or what events should fit into a certain stage.

- What calls for change are presenting themselves to you right now?
- Are there calls from your past that you have ignored or refused? Do they still call out to you?
- What stories are you telling yourself? Are they true or simply comforting?
- Whom did you look to for direction when you were growing up?
- Are there others who acted directly or indirectly as teachers or coaches?
- Would life be different if you hadn't met these people?
- How could your life be different if you had a coach or mentor?

Stage One: The Ordinary World

- Try to remember a time in your life when you were living your life and seemingly things were fine but you felt a small inkling that something wasn't quite right and there was something more out there for you.
- Detail the date and time in your life and describe what was going on in your life at this time.

Example:

I was living in suburbia with my 2 kids and a wife. I was working my ass off to get ahead and make a good life for my family. I wasn't exercising or eating a good diet and I was becoming miserable. I began to think something in my life had to change...

Your Turn:

_____

_____

_____

Stage Two: Call to Adventure

- Now that you have established your ordinary world, follow through your timeline to when something happened in your life that woke you up and got your attention. This can be a hardship like a job loss, divorce, loss of a loved one, or it can be something that you just woke up one day and knew you had to make a change in your life.

Example:

I was in the shower when I heard a voice say "This is not the way to live your life, you must be doing something wrong."...

Your Turn:

_____

_____

_____

Stage Three: Refusal of the Call

- List the time in your life where you heard the call to adventure but were too afraid or confused to follow through and make a change in your life.

Example:

I repeatedly refused the call. After I heard the call in the shower that morning it would be another nine years before I would fully answer the call, enter my new world by getting a divorce, being let go from my job of 16 years and starting my own business...

Your Turn:

_____

_____

_____

Stage Four: Meeting with the Mentor

- Who has been a mentor to you in your life? These can be people who you admired or learned from either before your call to adventure or after. As you progress through your journey you may lean on these mentors heavily or acquire new ones.

Example:

Through the years I've hired many therapists and coaches to help me move through the stuck times in life or to help boost my businesses. But I've also gleaned a great deal of wisdom from books or seminars that I've attended to aid me on my journey...

Your Turn:

_____

_____

_____

Is your Ego prepared for the journey?

Now that you have created your preparation phase stages answer the following questions to help you decide if your Ego has progressed in a healthy developmental way. Don't be critical if you still need work in this area, most of us do.

- Do you find yourself continuously doing things so others will like you or think you are okay?
- Do you have a hard time delegating? Do you feel you must run everything by yourself?
- Do you have a hard time accepting other peoples wishes or truths even if they conflict with yours?
- Are you afraid to say what you think because someone might get angry or are you afraid to leave a relationship or a job for fear that you can't make it on your own?
- Do you have a hard time accepting constructive criticism?
- Are you taking care of everyone in your family or office except yourself?

These answers should allow you to pinpoint areas that you may need to continue to work on before or as you move into the journey and return phases. They may also show you areas that you might want to change or add to your above stages.

Stage Five: Crossing the Threshold

- Review your timeline and find the time in your life where you finally said enough with this old way of thinking or living and actually made a change in your life. You were finally able to move out of your comfort zone and start something new or end something that needed ending and it changed your life in a new direction.
- If you can't think of a time when you feel you've crossed the threshold, then maybe you are still refusing the call or still in your ordinary life. That's okay, try and imagine a future timeline for your hero's journey and use it as a catalyst to move forward in your life.

Example:

My initial crossing the threshold came after I said to hell with all the doctors and physical therapists. At this point I wasn't sure what to do other than try to chill out...

Your Turn:

_____

_____

_____

Stage Six: Tests, Allies, and Enemies

- Now that you've crossed the threshold and living in the new unfamiliar special world, identify any trials and tribulations you went through as you moved through this new and unfamiliar territory.
- List friends and allies that appeared during this time that helped you get through these times. Also list or describe any enemies that you needed to face down. Enemies can also be difficult situations that you had to overcome.

Example:

After my divorce I started a new career as a professional portrait photographer. Now that all my old familiar friends from the marriage and my work were gone, I had to forge out and meet new friends and allies...

Your Turn:

_____

_____

_____

Stage Seven: The Approach

- Define a time in your life when you went into planning or strengthening or learning mode. This is a time in your life where you were in the thick of life. You are living in the new world and preparing to grow stronger physically, emotionally or both. You may not have known it at the time but you were preparing for even harder times ahead.
- This can be a very good time in your life when you felt like you were alive because you were moving forward.

Example:

As my consulting business was taking off I started to focus on my body and I began eating healthier and exercising more. I even went on a grain free diet and lost 40 pounds...

Your Turn:

_____

_____

_____

Stage Eight: The Ordeal

- Describe a time in your life where you had to face the scariest thing you've ever had to. Detail what it was, what you went through and the insights it brought.
- For some of us, there is more than one ordeal to identify. Just pick one at this time that fits with your timeline and hero's journey so far. There are other times in your journey where you will undergo trials and tribulations and have to face dragons and ogre's and you can list them there.

Example:

This stage for me was very long and painful. I have identified two parts of my life where I faced uphill battles and have named these my dark days...

Your Turn:

_____

_____

_____

Stage Nine: The Reward

- Identify a time in your life when you crossed the threshold, faced hardships (dragons) that you overcame and claimed victory. Be aware though, that there will be at least one more challenge to face on your journey home with the reward.

Example:

In October of the year I was diagnosed, I was declared cancer-free. I had conquered my fearful ordeal and won the battle with cancer. I was back on track living my life and consulting in Kansas...

Your Turn:

_____

_____

_____

Is your Soul prepared for the Return?

Now that you have completed the Journey phase, ask the following questions of yourself gently. As you build momentum, you can allow your fantasies to soar. Remember times when you felt satisfied or curious or content and allowed yourself to be fully present with all the sensations and images that fed your desires. Repeat each question until you have exhausted your answer: For example "I like _____ "Another thing I like is _____. Don't edit or critique your answers. Answer each question with the first words that pop into your head.

- I like
- I feel satisfied when
- I fully enjoy

- I want to do more
- I am happy when I
- What dreams do I have, day or night, that reveal my purpose?
- I feel fulfilled when I
- I feel curious about
- If I could change anything in my life I would change
- In my wildest fantasies, I have always wanted to
- List your gifts, talents and strengths
- What are my hidden gifts and talents?
- Now, review your list and decide which of these you can pass on to others
- Of all your gifts, talents and strengths, which is your best? What makes you stand out?
- What is your superpower?
- Are you willing to give up the life you've planned so you can have the life that is waiting for you?
- Where in your life are you playing defense? What would it look like to play some offense?
- Name one thing that you will do today that scares you.

These answers should allow you to pinpoint areas that you may need to continue to work on before you can move into the return phase and if you want to change any of your above Journey stages.

Stage Ten: The Road Back

- Identify a time in your life when you crossed the threshold, faced hardships (dragons) that you overcame and claimed victory. Be aware though, that there will be at least one more challenge to face on your journey home with the reward.
- This is a critical stage because you must return home after the victory. Remember a time in your life where you had achieved victory and were on the road back home to the ordinary world. Again, you will still be tested again before reaching home.

Example:

At this stage in my life the only chase scene I was experiencing was my dating failures and my chasing my tail trying to find true love again. I was trying various ways to find my girlfriend. From meetups to online dating to hanging out in bars with no success stories...

Your Turn:

_____

_____

_____

Stage Eleven: The Resurrection

- This may be the most interesting stage in the journey. It was for me at least. Just when you think you have defeated your dragons and claimed victory on your way home, you are severely tested one more time. Think of a time in your life where after a victory you were tested or faced one more challenge that purified you with one last lesson. Remember that even though this challenge may be the most severe, you have been on your hero's journey and have gained valuable insights, skills and mentors to help you face this last challenge.

Example:

I had been dating on and off since returning to Kansas but nothing was even remotely serious until one day out of the blue I met a women who would profoundly change the course of my life...

Your Turn:

_____

_____

_____

Stage Twelve: Return with the Treasure

- You finally made it back to your ordinary world with treasure in hand. You have gained much insight and strength during your journey. Your reward is either something tangible, like a new job, a relationship, renewed health or even more likely an amazing story of survival to tell your tribe.
- List a time where you found your true authentic self and were living your life purpose.

Example:

As I mentioned, this book is in part my return. Completing my hero's journey opened a whole new avenue of creativity for me. During my journey I encountered many mentors and healers and through meditation and journaling I realized that I have always had a sense to help people through education...

Your Turn:

_____

_____

_____

Have You Found Yourself?

- What is my personal kingdom, and what are my responsibilities to myself?
- What are my responsibilities to other people?
- Write a description of your role and responsibilities in the following areas of life:
    - Family
        -
    - Primary relationship
        -
    - Work
        -
    - Church or community group
        -
- Is it your turn to give back and pay it forward?
- Are you prepared to be a mentor?

Hero's Journey Summary

Now that you have broken down your life according the stages of the Hero's Journey it's time to put it all together and draw some conclusions. You want to figure out where in your life you have been the hero that was called to adventure, where you battled your metaphorical dragons and came out the victor. You also want to know where you refused the call. See if you can figure out why you refused the call for so long before you had the courage to cross the threshold and take your journey. What finally gave you the courage to move forward? Do you still have that courage today or have you lost it some how?

Review all of your stages and put together a few paragraphs of what you have gleaned by sorting your life into stages of the Hero's Journey. If you get on a roll and find yourself writing pages and pages, by all means go for it. This can be a very cathartic and eye opening experience. I know it was for me.

In latter exercises you will be identifying your limiting stories, beliefs and behaviors. You will want to use your Hero's Journey story to help identify those.

Example:

I started my adult life full of hope and passion. I wanted to live the American dream of owning a house in the suburbs, enjoying time with my wife and watching my kids grow up. What I didn't realize is that I was predisposed to general anxiety disorder and as I pursued the dream I was piling on heaps of stress and secreting stress producing hormones into my body with no escape. Basically I was in flight or fight all the time and the human body isn't made to function that way.

My Hero's Journey started when I heard the call to adventure in the shower one morning. But unfortunately it would be over 10 years before I would accept the call and cross the threshold into the unknown world.

My wake up call was getting laid off and divorced in the span of one year. The Universe knocked me on my ass.

I struggled for years in the unknown world drinking too much and feeling lonely and then getting cancer. But I rallied and healed and made a comeback by helping others and writing about my experiences in life.

After I returned from my journey and claimed victory, I took up the mantle of mentor and wrote this book and started life coaching to help people with life's challenges and helping them move forward as I did.

As this journey ends I embark on a new Hero's Journey as I build my business and foster a life time relationship with the women I love.

Your Turn:

_____

_____

_____

The Transformational Ladder

No matter if you are stuck in the middle of your Hero's Journey or have completed many Hero's Journey's there is always room for improvement. Human suffering comes from the illusion that we are not enough. This is universal for humans and it starts in young childhood when we are completely at the mercy of our parents to support us in life.

The transformational ladder will guide you from defining your limiting behaviors, down through the limiting stories you tell yourself, and what emotions are causing the main limiting beliefs that were created by original life triggering events. With this information, you will be ready to move onto climbing back up the ladder with new empowering beliefs, emotions, stories and behaviors, and become the hero of your life.

The exercises below will help you figure out where you are stuck in life and will give you insight on how to get unstuck and move forward in your journey. If you have completed the exercises in section one on the Hero's Journey, you can already see how your life has unfolded into your journey. Now it's time to go deep and define what you want to change in your life and why. It's your job to look back on your life and figure out where things may have gone wrong or where unfortunate circumstances took place, and what meaning you attached to those life events. As you use the exercises to uncover your personal growth pattern, you will begin to see yourself as the hero of your own life and how your life has shaped your journey so far. With this knowledge, you will peel back the onion of your transformational ladder and sit with this knowledge for a while. With a clear understanding of how your past life might have contributed to your limiting beliefs and actions, you will rebuild your ideal hero life by climbing back up the ladder with new and more empowering stories, feelings, thoughts and emotions.

Uncovering Where You Are Stuck

Where are you stuck in your life? These are areas where you are most frustrated, annoyed, disappointed, feeling helpless. The primary feelings of being stuck are powerlessness, hiding, and frustration.

Remember the first step to change is admitting you are stuck.

Some examples are:

- Stuck in a relationship you know isn't working.
- Stuck in a job that is sucking the life out of you.
- Maybe you have lost your connection to your faith.
- You never have enough money
- You are overweight
- You are out of shape
- Your family doesn't support you
- You have chronic pain

List Where You Are Stuck:

1.
2.
3.
4.
5.

Now take a few minutes to reflect on these stuck areas of your life above by answering the following questions.

- **How have you ignored these stuck areas or used them as excuses?**
  -
  -
  -

- **How long have these stuck areas been with you? Are you repeating a pattern?**
  -
  -
  -

- **Can you remember the first time when you felt stuck in these areas?**
  -
  -
  -

- **Do you believe that staying stuck in these areas benefited you in any way?**
  -
  -
  -

- Do you have any relationships in your life that support you being stuck in these areas?
  -
  -
  -

Why Must You Change?

Now let's get clear on why you must change. What have you missed out on because you let fear and apathy rule your life?

List them here. I have missed:

- **Romance:**
  -
- **Career:**
  -
- **Health:**
  -
- **Spirituality:**
  -
- **Relationships:**
  -
- **Finances:**
  -
- **Contribution:**
  -
- **Add Your Own Category:**

Make a list of all the things you want in your life. What do you want to feel? What do you want to do with your life? What things do you want to have in your life? Who do you want to love?

1.
2.
3.

4.

5.

Write out why you must commit to changing now (Be as detailed as possible.)

_____

_____

_____

_____

Now answer these questions:

- **What is the worst that could happen if I don't change now?**
  -
  -

- **What's the worst thing that could happen if I decide to change now?**
  -
  -

- **Has the Universe/God/Creator tried to get my attention recently? What were the signs?**
  -
  -

Now that you have identified where you are stuck, why you must change and what you want out of life, you will dive into your emotions, and what limiting beliefs, stories and events have held you back.

The difference between a belief, an emotion, a story and a behavior is when you have an early trauma or crisis in your life, a belief is the meaning that you created from that traumatic event. Beliefs create emotions or a felt sense in the body. Your emotions create your stories or how you describe your circumstances. Your stories create your behaviors or how you repeatedly react to your circumstances.

We are wired to assign meaning to what happens to us in life. The amazing thing, though, is that no one else can assign meaning to our life events, only we can do that. That should make you feel very very hopeful.

Your Limiting Stories, Thinking and Beliefs

What Are The Stories You Tell Yourself?

Our behaviors are usually driven by the stories we tell ourself. We don't just do things randomly. Our thoughts create our behavior. Every behavior was first a thought or story.

There are all kinds of stories that hold you back. Common ones are:

- The world is not a safe place
- I'm too old
- I'm too fat
- I don't have enough time
- I don't have enough money
- I'm too young
- I'm not safe
- Life will never get better
- This is all I'm worth
- I've always been this way
- I don't feel I can be my true self
- My children's happiness is more important than my own
- My parents don't approve of who I am
- Life doesn't support me
- I'm cursed
- This works for other people but not me.

You may see your stories above or have different ones. What stories are you telling yourself?

Write them down.

1.
2.
3.
4.
5.

Where did your limiting stories came from? As you do this, remember not to beat yourself up. Be kind and and gentle with yourself as you look at the hard parts of your life, and trust the process. Go back and read what you wrote about the stories you tell yourself. Allow yourself to soak them in.

Don't push them away.

Then ask yourself, where was the first time I remember hearing this story?

Some examples are:

- My parents
- Significant others
- Religion
- Bosses
- Brothers or sisters
- The media
- Bullies in school
- Your friends
- Extended family members
- People you look up to
- Role models
- Negative voices in my head

Then try and think about the actual words that these people said to you.

Some examples are:

- Finish your plate, there are starving kids in India
- You'll never amount to anything
- You're be just like your mother/father
- Children should be seen and not heard
- No one in this family has ever gone to college, what makes you think you can?
- Don't every air your dirty laundry in public

List your top 5 times when you first heard these limiting stories and what they were.

1.
2.
3.
4.
5.

Identify Limiting Beliefs

Beliefs are more powerful than stories because beliefs are in many ways the origin of the stories we tell about life, because beliefs are based on the meaning we gave past events in our life. In other words, belief determines how we see or perceive and event. Like a filter. And a story is the account of what happened or what will happen based on your beliefs.

Some Examples Are:

- I'll never get a new job
- No one ever listens to me
- He always makes me feel angry
- Everyone uses me

- I want to call it quits
- Today is a bad day for me, so why bother trying to change it.
- It's her fault that my life is this way
- I'm really not that smart
- I honestly can't change. Maybe it would be better to start another time
- I don't feel like it
- My life sucks
- I hate my situation with _____
- I'll never make a difference. I can't
- _____ does not like me
- I have to work harder than most people.
- It's my genetics. I am just like my mother

Review the stories you tell yourself and where they came from and turn them into belief statements.

List your limiting beliefs here:

1.
2.
3.
4.
5.

Uncovering Your Triggering Life Events

We are going to go back to a time of hurt, a time you have pushed away for so long, a time that you may even have pretended didn't happen and that you don't want to talk about. It is your moment or moments of trauma, pain and original hurt.

These triggering life events are moments in our past when something happened and we decided to form a belief about the world. They come from all kinds of places. They can be something as simple as being left behind at school, a kid calling you fat, or the tone in which a parent said something to you as a child. Or your they could be more extreme, like sexual, emotional, or physical abuse.

The majority of these triggering life events start before the age of 10. Because they are never addressed or worked through, these limiting beliefs carry themselves into adulthood. In order to change your story these triggering life events must be seen with new eyes. It's time to uncover how these limiting beliefs were created to protect yourself long ago and step into your more powerful life. It may take running through this process a few times to find all the triggering life events.

Here is a list of common triggering life events.

- Sexual abuse
- Physical abuse
- Emotional abuse
- Violent family members
- Being required to be perfect, rather than yourself
- Being abandoned by on for both parents
- A parents addiction
- Needed to be the caregiver of your parent as a child
- Other people condemning you
- Being made fun of at school
- Witnessing violence
- The death of a loved one
- Not being recognized by your father
- Not being nurtured by your mother

Go back and read your top five limiting beliefs. Take a minute to let the emotions to wash over you.

Then ask yourself "What triggering life events happened in my life that made me believe these things?"

1.
2.

3.

4.

5.

Your Negative Emotions

Go back to the list you created of the limiting thinking, stories and beliefs that hold you back. Reread them. Then bring your awareness to your body. How are you feeling as you read these stories, thoughts and beliefs? And where are you feeling it? Some people feel these deep strong emotions in there stomach, jaw or weakness in the legs. Pay attention to where you feel them.

Right now we are just going to sit with those feelings rather than acting on them. If this brings up panic, fear and shame, that is okay. There is nothing wrong with you. Remember you are not your feelings and emotions.

I usually feel my deep emotions in my throat and solar plexus. Where do you feel your deep emotions?

Think of all the times your limiting stories, thoughts and beliefs that have held you back. Look at the pain you've caused others. Look at the pain you've caused yourself. Look how you have kept yourself small, how you've put others first, denied your own worth and intuition. Look back over your hero's journey life and see how you've held yourself back. Notice how this makes you feel and where you feel it in your body.

Naming Your Emotions

Now that you have gotten in touch with your emotions list five emotions that you feel as a result of these limiting behaviors and stories and the areas in your body where you feel them.

If it's hard to access your emotions, or if you're getting frustrated that you aren't feeling anything, this is good. You're feeling frustrated. Where do you feel that in your body? Just because you don't feel the emotions you think you should be feeling doesn't mean you can't feel. Your job is to go with whatever is present in the here and now.

Some common emotions are:

- Anger
- Hate, Powerlessness
- Guilt
- Shame
- Sadness
- Unworthiness
- Betrayal
- Regret
- Depression
- Stress
- Self-doubt
- Lack of belonging
- Resentment

List your emotions here:

1. I feel _____ in my _____
2. I feel _____ in my _____
3. I feel _____ in my _____
4. I feel _____ in my _____
5. I feel _____ in my _____

These are difficult things to feel, and you may want to turn back. But don't. Stay with it. These feelings will pass and fade away. These emotions do not control you. In fact, feeling them is the first step toward setting yourself free

Identify Limiting Thinking

Next ask yourself - How do I think when I feel this way? For example if you want to get rid of the feeling of shame. Ask yourself "What is my attitude when I feel shame?" You might say you are scared or timid or quiet and shy. An attitude is a series of thoughts connected to a feeling. You need to define the habit that has been created by this emotion.

Some Examples Are:

- Competitive
- Blaming
- Desperate
- Lacking
- Overly intellectual
- Lazy
- Dishonest
- Controlling
- Needy
- Sensitive
- Insensitive

List your top 5.

1.
2.
3.
4.
5.

Most of your actions, behaviors and choices have been equal to these feelings and has made you act in predictable ways. Just be with these emotional attitudes without doing anything. Just observe them.

<u>Limiting Behaviors That Hold You Back</u>

The difference between a belief, an emotion, a story and a behavior is when you have an early trauma or crisis in your life, a belief is the meaning that you created from that traumatic event. Beliefs create emotions or a felt sense in the body. Your emotions create your stories or how you describe your circumstances. Your stories create your behaviors or how you repeatedly react to your circumstances.

We are wired to assign meaning to what happens to us in life. The amazing thing, though, is that no one else can assign meaning to our life events, only we can do that. That should make you feel very very hopeful.

List the 5 behaviors that hold you back. These are the behaviors you blame yourself for doing and yet you can't seem to find a way past them.

Some of these behaviors might be:

- Self-sabotage
- Over-eating
- Blaming Others
- Withdrawing or hiding
- Lying
- Abusing porn
- Abusing gambling
- Cheating on your partner

List your limiting behaviors here:

1.
2.
3.
4.
5.

Admitting Who You Are

Acknowledge your true self rather than the self you show to other people. Allow yourself to be vulnerable. Tell the Universe/God/Creator who you have been and what you want to change about yourself, and admit what you are hiding.

Owning up to who we really are and what our past mistakes have been and asking to be accepted are among the most challenging things for us to do as humans. This works because we are admitting our faults and failures to our higher power and not to another similarly flawed human.

Close your eyes and become still and begin to tell this higher power who you have been. Share the details of the stories that you have carried around with you.

Some Examples Are:

- I am afraid of falling in love because it hurts too much
- I pretend I am happy, but I am really suffering because I am lonely
- I do not want anyone to know that If feel so guilty, so I lie about myself
- I lie to people so that they like me and so I won't feel so unloved and unworthy.
- I can't stop feeling self-pity. I think, act, and feel this way all day long because I do not know how else I can feel.
- I have felt like a failure most of my life, so I try extra to be a success

Write down what comes up.

_____

_____

_____

_____

Creating The New You - Climbing Back Up The Transformational Ladder

Up till now you've worked at identifying your limited thinking and pruning away old synaptic connections. Now it's time to sprout new ones so that the new mind you create will become the platform of who you will be in your future. Let's find your bliss and create a new you. Your daily meditations, contemplations, and rehearsals will be like tending to a garden to yield a great expression of the new you. You should fall in love with the vision of who you are becoming. Love is a higher frequency emotion than those in survival emotions that allowed the negative and limiting beliefs to control your unconscious thinking.

Below are a series of open ended questions that will cause you to think in different ways than you normally think and to entertain new possibilities, - This turns on your frontal lobe. You are creating the platform of the new self by forcing the brain to fire in novel ways.

Write down answers to as many questions seems relevant to you. After you complete the answers, review, reflect, analyze and think about all the possibilities your answers raise. You will then be climbing the transformational ladder with new beliefs, emotions, stories and behaviors.

How Do I Want To Think

- What is the greatest ideal of myself?
-
-

- Who in history do I admire?
-
-

- Whom do I want to model?
  -
  -

- How would I be if I were like them?
  -
  -

- What would I say to myself if I were this new person I want to be?
  -
  -

- How would I talk to others if I were changed.
  -
  -

How Do I Want To Act?

- How would this new person act?
  -
  -

- What would I do?
  -
  -

- How do I see myself behaving?
  -
  -

- How would I speak as this new expression of self?
  -
  -

- What is my new attitude?
  -
  -

- What do I want to believe about me?
  -
  -

- How do I want to be perceived?
  -
  -

- What would I say to myself if I was this person?
  -
  -

- How would this person act?
  -
  -

- What would he or she do?
  -
  -

- How do I see myself behaving?
  -
  -

- How would I speak as this new person?
  -
  -

How Do I Want To Feel?

- How would this new self be?
    -
    -

- What would I feel?
    -
    -

- What would my energy be like as this new ideal?
    -
    -

Now that you have brainstormed how you want to think, feel and act differently, it's time to get specific on your new empowering stories, beliefs, thinking and behaviors.

Review you limiting stories, beliefs, thinking and behaviors and rewrite them into positives statements.

New Empowering Stories That Move Your Forward

List your top 5.

1.
2.
3.
4.
5.

New Empowering Beliefs That Move Your Forward

List your top 5:

1.
2.
3.
4.
5.

New Empowering Thinking That Move Your Forward

List your top 5:

1.
2.
3.
4.
5.

New Empowering Behaviors That Move Your Forward

List your top 5:

1.
2.
3.
4.
5.

<u>Hero Life Exercise:</u>

Step 1: What is Your Hero Moment?

Imagine a time in your life when you accomplished or did something that made you feel absolutely incredible. A time where you felt empowered, confident, happy, and full of energy. A time in your life that you felt like you can do anything you put your mind to.

It can be ANY time in your life. When you were a kid, hitting a home run, acing a test, leaving your job, getting a big check, accomplishing something significant, falling in love, speaking on stage, or doing something you've never done before and crushing it.

_____

_____

_____

_____

Step 2: Refine it, what was the most powerful part of your hero life moment?

Refine it all the way down to one specific moment. Examples: receiving an award, the feeling of crossing home plate after the game winning home run, the sound of the crowd during a standing ovation, the feeling of looking at an "A" on your final exam.

_____

_____

_____

_____

Step 3: Attach a meaning to it, why is that moment so significant for you?

What does it mean to you? Examples, you accomplished something great before and you can do it again. You stepped outside your comfort zone and you can do it again. You can do anything you put your mind to.

_____

_____

_____

_____

Step 4: Physiologically how did you feel during your Hero moment?

What did you feel, how did you stand, how were you breathing, what did you hear?

_____

_____

_____

_____

If you can have that happen to you back then, what is holding you back now? What if you could achieve something this amazing now?

What if you thought about this moment every day and recreated that physiological response in your body? You can leverage this for any project, event or anytime you want to get pumped up empowered to take action.

Discovering Purpose and Passion

Passion and purpose are similar but distinct. They are connected and seductive to us all.

The following exercises will help draw out the purpose and passion that resides within you. Don't come at this with preconceived ideas of what your purpose is or should be or what others think it should be.

Take your time with these questions. The answers you seek will be revealed when you go inward with calmness, patience and vulnerability.

Think about what makes you tear up?

- When you are emotionally moved, it is a sign of what resonates within you, either good or bad, happy or sad. We all have something that triggers our emotions and feelings. Describe what that is for you.

_____

_____

_____

_____

What makes you angry and annoyed?

- What kinds of things make you really mad and sometimes pushes you over the top?
- When you declare what makes you angry you are leaving clues as to what you are passionate about.

_____

_____

_____

_____

What charges and recharges you?

- What inspires and motivates you?
- Is it nature? Is it when you are being creative? Do you like working in groups or by yourself? Does music inspire you? What kind?
- The answers to this question are closely connected to your purpose and passion.

_____

_____

_____

_____

What are you better at than anyone else you know?

- This is when you are in your flow zone and quite often lose track of them when you're doing this.

_____

_____

_____

_____

What can people count on you to always do?

- In your family, what is it that you always do?
- At work, what are you the go to person for?
- This is where you walk your talk and find it easy to do.
- People have been telling you this your whole life.

_____

_____

_____

_____

When will you be worthy?

- What needs to happen for you to feel truly worthwhile? Remember we are hardest on ourselves.
- How will you know when you have "arrived?" When will your credibility be irrefutable?

_____

_____

_____

_____

What gift will you share with the world?

- Think about where your pain and suffering lives.
- Think about the areas that you want to hide .
- It may also be connected to your deepest desires.

_____

_____

_____

_____

Who or what would you die for?

- What means the most you? Who would you make the ultimate sacrifice for?
- When you know what you would die for it grants you the wisdom of knowing what to live for.
- Think about what's in it for you?

_____

_____

_____

_____

When your time is up what would your final wish be?

- You're not allowed to ask for more time.
- How will you use it?
- What will it be for?
- Who will benefit?
- When all you have is one wish left, your answer will be very revealing. Your purpose and passion are rooted in your values.

_____

_____

_____

_____

How do you want to be remembered?

- When you think about this, what would honor your memory the most?
- What stories would you most like to hear told about you at your funeral?
- The answers to this question are what are most important to you. These are the traits and attributes you value the most in life.
- This is how you want to live your life

_____

_____

_____

_____

Your passion and purpose are in these answers. You are the hero of your own life.

Rehearsing The New You

You've unpacked your limiting thinking, figured out why and created new empowering thinking as you climbed back up the transformational ladder. You have figured out your mission and what you're passionate about. Now it's time to take these new empowering views, follow your bliss and create the hero of your life. This part of the exercise will include creating powerful daily personal meditations and contemplations.

- Hold the image of you being or doing the things that you want this new you to do. You are the quantum observer, commanding matter to conform to your intentions.
- With clarity, hold the image of each manifestation in your mind for a few seconds, and then let it go into the quantum to be executed by a great mind.
- Give up trying to figure out how or when or where or with whom, leave those details to a mind that knows so much more than you do. And know that your creation will come in a way that you will least expect so that will surprise you and leave no doubt that this came from a higher order.

When you are unconsciously skilled at something, that means you just do it without having to place a great deal of conscious thought or attention to the activity. This is what you want to have happen. You want to practice being the new you so much that it becomes unconscious. The keys for you to focus on are Frequency, Intensity, and Duration. The more you do it, the easier it gets. The better you can focus and concentrate, the easier it will be for you to tap into that particular mind the next time. The longer you can linger in the thoughts, and emotions of your new ideal, without letting your mind wander to extraneous stimulus the more you will memorize new thoughts and feelings.

Creating A New Reality

Your new personality should create a new reality. When you are being someone else, you naturally will have a different life. The new identity is no longer emotionally anchored to known situations in your life that keep recycling the same circumstances; therefore it is a perfect place from which to envision a new destiny. This is the place you want to be to create your hero life.

The reason your past intensions hardly every manifested is that you were trying to hold a mindful intention while being lost in lower emotions such as guilt, shame, sadness, unworthiness, anger or fear connect to the old self. It was those feelings that were governing your thoughts and attitude. The 5% of your conscious mind was fighting against the 95% subconscious. Thinking one way and feeling another cannot produce results.

Creating a New Destiny

Now that you have released that old energy from the body, what do you want? Do you want to heal an area of you body or life? Do you want a loving relationship, a more satisfying career, a new car? Is your dream to write a book, to send your kids to college or yourself go back to school? From a new state of mind, body and gratitude; in a greater more coherent energy, see these images in your mind of what you want to create in your new life. Craft the specific future events you want to experience, by observing them into physical reality. You as the quantum observer are commanding matter to conform to your intentions. With clarity you will hold the image of each manifestation in your mind for a few seconds, and the let it go into the quantum field to be executed by your Universe/God?Creator.

Finally, give up trying to figure out how or when or where or with whom. Leave those details to a mind that nows so much more than you do. And know that your creation will come in a way that you will least expect, that will surprise you and leave no doubt that it came from a higher mind.

Write down what you want now that you are the new you.

- _____
- _____
- _____
- _____

It might be helpful to create 6 month goals from this list. By putting dates on when you expect to have or be these new ideas you are giving the quantum field even more information to help it manifest with you. Of course you still need to be surprised as to how or even when these events will occur. In fact these areas might be manifested way before your goal date.

Again, be as specific as you can be in what you want so you can visualize it and feel the joy and emotion of having achieved it in your life.

You are now ready to start your meditations. Now that you have worked through the transformational ladder, created a new you and made your six months goals, it's now time to put it all together into one mediation that you can do every day.

Pick one emotion (at a time) and associated thoughts, feelings, actions and behaviors that you want to be rid of. Remind yourself of the emotions, feelings and behaviors you use to think and feel and ask the creator to take this emotion away from you. You can find this list in your Transformational Ladder exercises.

Hero Life

www.herolifetoday.com

Hero life is J. Scott's coaching and education business. We specialize in helping people become their true authentic and mission driven selves through coaching and education programs.

CPSIA information can be obtained
at www.ICGtesting.com
Printed in the USA
LVHW090104060819
626670LV00001B/67/P

9 781982 216429